THE COMPLETE LIGHT POEMS
of
Jackson Mac Low

THE COMPLETE
LIGHT POEMS
1 – 60

Jackson Mac Low

Edited by Anne Tardos & Michael O'Driscoll

chax press
victoria texas 2015

ISBN 978 0 9862640 0 9 Paperback Edition
ISBN 978 0 9862640 1 6 Special Handbound Boxed Edition

Funding for this book includes generous support from
the Publishing Program of the University of Houston-Victoria.

Special thanks to Sarah Caitlin Ghusson for her assistance in the preparation of the manuscript
leading to the production of this book.

Cover Design by Anne Tardos

Chax Press
PO Box 162
Victoria, TX 77902-0162
http://chax.org

CONTENTS

PREFACE

Jackson Mac Low's *Complete Light Poems* appear exactly ten years after the poet's death. The first *22 Light Poems* were published by Black Sparrow Press in 1968. In the ensuing 20 years, Jackson wrote 38 more Light Poems, ending with the "60th Light Poem: In Memoriam Robert Duncan, 8–9 October 1988." The Light Poems, begun in 1962, are unique to Mac Low's body of work in that they were written intermittently, over a period of 26 years.

Michael O'Driscoll, co-editor of this book, who wrote the important essay "By the Numbers: Jackson Mac Low's Light Poems and Algorithmic Digraphism,"[1] met with me at the Jackson Mac Low archive at the Mandeville Special Collections at the University of California at San Diego, where we were able to locate all of Jackson's Light Poems—we hope. Many of these poems are unknown, unpublished, and in some cases, incomplete. We found changes and corrections, and in one case, a crayon-scratched-out and abandoned "39th Light Poem for Kathy Acker"— included here. The reason for the poem's condition is undocumented, but we know that Jackson wrote other poems and performance scores for her, most notably the "Black Tarantula Crossword Gathas."

Among the newly discovered Light Poems, I am particularly interested in the 48th for Rochelle Owens. Unique to this poem is Jackson's use of the typewriter as instrument-specific: "*& amybe means maybe.*" Here, misspellings are freely allowed into the poem, in fact, those very typos become central to the poem's material and syntax in an enlightened improvisation: "Mahlet means Mahler it means his 3rd Symphony" or "Heatwavetyping Lnaguage: interript means interrupt has lowered to means have lowered the Lnaguage means Language. (God rest Jack Spicer.)"[2]

In contrast, I think of my own writings, which are typically composed directly on the computer, and where improvisation comes less from the instrument, than from the speed at which I can write. The rapid transcription of thought into type, allows for spontaneity of thought. Ideas are gently coaxed, and almost always come as a surprise.

What interests me in Mac Low's Light Poems and other personal poems like the Odes, is an immediacy and directness, where technique and procedural methods become secondary to the poem's totality. Transparency and quotidian observations expose the reader to profound insights. Reading the Light Poems, we become intimately familiar with details of the poet's life over the years, and we are privy to a chronological archiving. These poems are a platform for expressing love, affection, admiration, disappointments, and resentments; working through disputes fueled by anger, examining and disclosing Mac Low's political and philosophical views. At times tenderly, but always candidly, he addresses his dedicatee(s) as well as himself, and always mindful of us, the readers. Jerome Rothenberg once described Mac Low as "reporting the world to us with a cranky accuracy."

In the Light Poems, Mac Low often engaged in lengthy digressions, at the end of which he once wrote "How is all this getting into this Light Poem?" This nine-word line, again, makes me think of one of my own lines from my Nines: "Take a nap in the middle of a Nine?" or "And why am I writing everything in nines, anyway," and "One more line and we're done with this Nine."

I have often wondered where self-referential writing ends and objective observation begins. Endearingly, Mac Low continually invites us into the time and place of his writing. We are, as it were, being let in from the cold: "Just me & the cats & and the plants I just took a shower it's not quite 100 degrees here."

Mac Low was confident that these poems were of great importance, not only in personal, but in artistic historical terms. Still, his humility and humor shine through when reading the 29th for Olson—one has to smile, as Jackson describes himself, sitting between the two giants, Olson and Rexroth, as "a chipmunk between two grizzly bears . . . often seeming overbearing boors / to my melancholy, reticent, twenty-six-year-old self . . ."

Many of the poems are not without irony. At the end of the 10-page Light Poem for Gustav Mahler, he decides not to end the poem with the self-important phrase "Action-accomplishing Wisdom." Especially the word "Wisdom" at the bottom of page 9: "Wow," he writes, "whatta way to end a poem: 'The Green Light of Action-Accomplishing
Wisdom'
What phoney baloney. What do I know about 'Action-Accomplishing Wisdom' or any other kinda 'Wisdom' or even just wisdom?" . . .

He then writes another page and ends the poem in mid-sentence, at the bottom of page 10, leaving us with a comma:

      "The red

         light

                of the skandha of perception

                                     in its basic

         puri-

      ty,"

On March 1, 1999, Jackson wrote the following lines:

        The necessity of ending is not the necessity of beginning.

        How finely is that said.

        An end of a play is not the end of a day.

        After giving

I note that the last line does not end with a period.[3]

The last poem we know of, the 60th for Duncan, in memoriam, ends with these wonderful lines:

      Gone

          gone

               gone

      Gone

          gone

               gone

      Not the end—

        Grandma brought Hermes Trismegistus to the West

          in a covered wagon.

I heard Jackson read this poem in public several times, and remember the audience falling silent at the series of "gone's," which he read slowly and gravely—as it is typed—with long pauses between the words, six times. Everyone expected "gone" to be the end of the poem, until Jackson suddenly read the last two lines, rapidly and upbeat, which always got terrific laughs. The audience was relieved and liberated by this zany humor, something Jackson shared with Duncan.

The Light Poems were not written lightly. To have a Light Poem written for you by Jackson, was something special. As one of the dedicatees, I am thankful to have been so lovingly addressed.

My profound gratitude and appreciation to Michael O'Driscoll for co-editing this collection with dedication and devotion. His understanding of Mac Low's work—and especially the Light Poems, is extraordinary. My gratitude to Charles Alexander for his generosity in publishing this book, and for coming up with the idea of doing so, at the same time that I was contemplating it myself. I thank Lynda Claassen and the archivists of the Mandeville Collection for their generous hospitality. For the long friendship and loving support of Diane and Jerome Rothenberg I am most grateful. My husband, Michael Byron's powerful support throughout, and meticulous editorial input were nothing short of indispensable. I thank him.

—Anne Tardos, 2014

1   *Time in Time: Short Poems, Long Poems, and the Rhetoric of North American Avant-Gardism*, 1963–2008. ed. J. Mark Smith (McGill-Queens University Press, Montreal, 2013)

2   From the "48th Light Poem for Rochelle Owens"

3   The poem was found among Jackson's papers in 2005, without any other information than the signature, followed by the date. It was reproduced on the back of the program of the "Memorial for and Tribute to Jackson Mac Low, at the Poetry Project at St. Mark's Church in New York, March 5th, 2005."

Introduction

For one eventful week in July, 2013 I had the singular honor of joining poet and artist Anne Tardos, at the Mandeville Special Collections Library at UC San Diego, in a search for the unpublished Light Poems of her late husband Jackson Mac Low. At that point, only thirty-five of the sixty poems we suspected were extant had seen their way into public view, and we spent the week sifting through Mac Low's notebooks and typescripts in what was for me, even after two decades of archival sleuthing, the most exciting and moving research experience of my career. Anne was a wonderful research partner—enthusiastic and dedicated and, most of all, determined even under conditions that, a decade after his death, must have been quite difficult. Among the highlights of our week was a dinner (one of several) with Jerome and Diane Rothenberg. That evening, the guests in their welcoming home witnessed an impromptu reading of the "16th Light Poem," written for Armand Schwerner on a fretful day in August, 1962. The occasion of the poem, and the account that drew the Rothenbergs' attention, was an uncharitable reading by Schwerner of one of Mac Low's poems at a gathering at Jerry and Diane's home. Moved both to confront this slight and, at the same time, to gracefully preserve his friendship with Schwerner, Mac Low wrote one of the many Light Poems that would draw so poignantly from the immediacy of his everyday life. More than half a century later, as first Anne, and then Jerry, read from the poem, I had the sense that a sort of journey was nearing completion, and that these uncollected Light Poems that so deserve a central place in Mac Low's oeuvre were finally, in a sense, arriving at their destination. They had come full circle, crossed a continent, gathered together, and returned from the future to emerge into the light they so wonderfully celebrate.

And what a celebration that is: "citrine light," "moonlight," "naptha-lamp light." In addition to the sustained voice and extended focus of a genius poet, what holds these poems together is their varied use of a chart of light names constructed by Mac Low in 1962. At the time, Mac Low was working as an editorial assistant at Funk & Wagnall's when he rescued some useful looking documents from the garbage of his employer. In the fourteen columns and twenty rows of an editorial department payroll form, and drawing from the pages of a Funk & Wagnall's dictionary, Mac Low charted 288 kinds of light, providing the basis for a creative process that varied with shifts in mood and moment. The result is a sustained meditation on a theme, and reading these poems one comes to an attunement to the word, and to the concept, and to a history of "light" that might otherwise be elusive. Following Mac Low's own keen observations, one sees light, hears light, experiences light in a manner that I suspect for most of us is anything other than typical. That attunement is an effect of repetition: light, light, light, light, light. Reiterative, cumulative, compulsive, a mantra of sorts. The light chart, taken as a whole, is the generative matrix and visual sum of this entire project. Any one of its coordinates alone—"lilac light," "sunbeam," "illucidation," "chandelier," "sparkle"—means little, would have little effect, except for its configuration in relation to all the others, except for its actuation in the form of these poems.

Over the years, the light chart went astray on a number of occasions. Misplaced in the jumble of Mac Low's papers and books, it was lost, found, lost again, and at one point imagined stolen and gone for good. Nonetheless, that chart is still in Anne's possession, and we've reproduced it, in all its resplendence, with the end matter of this volume, where it accompanies Mac Low's own description of the methods of composition that generated these poems. What one sees in that chart is, foremost, a work of art that is both process and product. The patient project of a commitment to a system of excess that is itself golden hued and richly luminous, the chart has a kind of complex beauty that, one might say, is a hallmark of Mac Low's most compelling work. And, indeed, what one sees in this schema of antiquated, scientific, philosophical, natural, and idiomatic names of light is a charting of the history, ideas, and language gathered around the centrality of illumination to our everyday lives. In "arc light" one cannot but recall the wonder with which electric light ushered in modernity; in "cinematographic light" the moving image and the art of contingency; in "Aufklärung" the history of enlightenment thought; in "radioactivity" and "napalm flame" the horror of the last century; in "Magellanic cloud light" the constitution of form and being in light; in "naked light" the erotics of the colloquial.

The poems are remarkable on many and various counts, but what I'd like to focus on here are the qualities that, it might be argued, constitute the Light Poems as an exceptional contribution to late twentieth-century American poetry: their extraordinary duration, their celebration of the quotidian and contingent, and their singularity of genre—if such a thing might be possible.

The sixty poems in this collection were written over an extended stretch of the poet's life, beginning on June 10, 1962 and concluding on October 9, 1988, more than twenty-six years later. The poems, then, were begun by Mac Low aged 39 and completed or, perhaps, left off, when he was 66 years old. As the work of an accomplished artist at mid life, the poems express a certain self-confidence and maturity at the same time as they are all too vulnerable in their frank recognition of the frailties of self and love. The Light Poems are often very moving. For that reason, and given their intensely biographical nature, the poems afford the reader an unusually prolonged and intimate sense of the poet's daily life. There is, however, no narrative arc here; rather, the Light Poems are a record of a life lived. For that, indeed, is the subject matter of the Light Poems: Mac Low's recordings are both commonplace and contingent—certainly everyday in spirit and immediate in their attention to the world around him. If the poems have a politics—and they most certainly do—it is at least partially in their insistence on the value of recorded private time and the marking of domestic space. The poems are also both idiosyncratic and immanent; they mark the import of experience outside the rationalizations of modernity and capital. And they record their progress on their own terms—a poem begun at 6:00 A.M. one morning, and completed at 2:00 A.M. the next, that attends to the passing of light across the kitchen walls, enumerates the sundry objects in view of the poet, registers the emotional response to music and radio banter, and meditates on the poet's own hopes and anxieties, does so as an assertion of the real value of all that will not be taken up by the commercial world of profit and exploitation.

There are, for example, the eight Light Poems written for Sharon Mattlin, the young woman with whom Mac Low found a renewed passion, for a time, in the wake of his marriage to Iris Lezak and before Anne Tardos became the love of his late life. Beginning with an extended sequence of thirty-one page-length odes in the 41st Light Poem, and concluding three and half years later with the 51st Light Poem, these dedications tell the story of Mac Low's relationship with Mattlin over several years. Opening (as it seems all relationships do) with ardent expressions of infatuation, reveling in explicitly erotic moments and emphatic in their loving declarations, Mattlin's Light Poems gradually diminish in intensity, introduce elements of doubt and worry, and end (in the 53rd Light Poem dedicated to Stephanie Vevers), with a declaration regarding Sharon: "I don't have to desire her any more." This is an astounding glimpse into some of the most private moments of Mac Low's life. But while the explicit and revealing nature of these poems is striking, perhaps what is just as significant here is their fervent attention to the banality of everyday life. In the summer month captured by the initial sequence of odes, we're witness to the details of Mac Low's kitchen and bedroom, passing time with pigeons in the backyard of Sharon's home, watching unremarkable television, writing and reflection, playing with the children, listening to Coltrane or Reich or the radio, and riding the trains. Love here, however extraordinary its passions, is woven into the fabric of ordinary life and becomes, thereby, a no greater or lesser thread in that rather familiar cloth.

And if love is quotidian, so also death. As the Light Poems progress, one of their increasingly important functions is to memorialize the dead. Although he'd died a year and a half earlier, the first of these memorial poems is for John Coltrane, written by Mac Low in January, 1969. In a poem, one could argue, that mimics the logic and spirit of that musician's styling, the 24th Light Poem encodes the letters of Coltrane's full name through reference to nuclei on the light chart while poignantly gathering around the question, "How can the howling void / be cheated of his light?" Mac Low, it seems, had discovered an important role that the Light Poems might play in their marking of the passing years. It is, however, with the death of Charles Olson in January, 1970, one year later, that Mac Low's use of the elegiac takes on fullest form. Here, in what becomes characteristic of his memorializations, Mac Low moves through engaging reminiscence and tangential narrative associations in the first half of the poem, while turning to the powerful "Litany of the Beautiful Lights" in the second. The poem, as presented here, was originally read at St. Mark's Church in-the-Bowery on February 4, 1970—and what a stunning moment that must have been. The elegiac function of these poems clearly became increasingly important to Mac Low. With the death of the much beloved Paul Blackburn in the fall of 1971, Mac Low abandoned and displaced the original 32nd Light Poem, a cosmic tribute to the "O & the B Stars," in favor of a new 32nd dedicated to his friend. Moving and tender in its account of Mac Low's lingering memories, the poem deftly invokes forms of light, the names of which silently spell out the letters of Paul Blackburn's name. It must have been a difficult time, for the next poem memorializes actor Leonard Hicks, who had passed away that August and for whom Mac Low expresses such warm admiration, while the 34th remembers the tragic death of Jennie Hecht. As in the case of the 24th for Coltrane, the 36th Light Poem for Buster Keaton occurs belatedly (as does the 49th for Gustav Mahler) but is likewise directed to a kindred spirit: Keaton as a performer and filmmaker—an absolute master of the art of light—who pairs physical comedy with the serious business of celebrating work itself, must have been an attractive subject for Mac Low. The poet Paul Goodman is remembered in the 42nd, his emotional and political commitments a measure for Mac Low's own, and then, to end the entire sequence, a remembrance for Robert Duncan, in a voice that itself resonates with quiet poignancy and a final sympathetic chuckle.

Many of the Light Poems, such as the 60th for Duncan, encode the names of their dedicatees in the text, inscribing a kind of love and fealty to which only the patience of such a laborious process might attest. Consider the 58th Light Poem for Anne Tardos: **a**ctinism, **n**oon light, **n**orthern lights, **e**vanescent light, **t**ranquil light, **a**ureole, **r**elucence, **d**eflected light, **o**rdinary light, **s**un. I won't repeat an account of the methods that Mac Low describes so clearly in the notes that conclude this volume, but as I have discussed elsewhere, this "paragrammatic" quality (to use Steve McCaffery's term) of Mac Low's writing silently encodes the generation of the text in a manner that at once gives shape to and disrupts the lyric expressiveness of the Light Poems. Although one might think of the light chart as "source text" and the dedicatee's name as "seed text," the Light Poems are not quite "diastic" in Mac Low's typical use of his coinage for "reading through." Rather, algorithmic, procedural, deterministic, quasi-intentional, nucleic: these are Mac Low's own words and the terms that best describe the amalgam of his methods here, which, while reminiscent of John Cage's mesostic poetries and other chance driven or non-egoic forms, work more explicitly in their "gathering" (another Mac Low term) to produce a tense dialectic that confounds the impossible poles of both purely intentional and aleatoric writing methods. When Charles Bernstein praises the "pluriform" force of Mac Low's writing, it is here in the Light Poems that one might most clearly recognize that multiplicity of method and that resistance to simple taxonomies that coerce and constrain us.

And it is the case that the Light Poems constitute the most formally and procedurally inclusive sequence of poems in Mac Low's oeuvre—"inclusive" in that the Light Poems range from the thirty-one expressive odes of the 41st Light Poem right through to the Gatha for Ian Tyson that is the 54th; from the performance instructions for Brecht (5th), Higgins (8th), Kaprow (30th), and Morrow (35th), to the weighty "found" text of John Martin's 21st Light Poem, a tribute that takes the absorptive, if unpredictable, turn of tracking recessive dictionary definitions around and through classical Greek religion and the Eleusinian mysteries. Eschewing narrative development and structural consistency, the Light Poems in their indifferent capaciousness are serial poems in the sense defined by Joseph Conte and comparable with the work of George Oppen's *Discrete Series,* Robert Duncan's *Passages*, Leslie Scalapino's *Way,* and Rachel Blau DuPlessis' *Drafts*, among many others. At the same time, however, there are echoes of Charles Olson's documentary collage (everywhere, but particularly in the citational 28th, 40th, and 53rd Light Poems), a mirroring of the loquacious spontaneity of David Antin's talk poetry (the 48th for Rochelle Owens stands out), and in the direct transcription of radio broadcasts (20th, 41st, 48th, and passim), an anticipation of the practices of contemporary conceptual poets. But even with such discontinuous accumulations, the Light Poems nonetheless do maintain the thematic consistency of light itself, bolstered by recurrent events of key import: the

1897 Parisian fire that killed 126 during a movie screening, a sighting of the Aurora Borealis during a trip to Nova Scotia in the summer of 1971, astrological prediction, cosmological science, technological discovery. Together these events weave together a life of love and friendship, creation and contemplation, strife and loss, in the polymathic sensibility of a modern mind. Loosely bound to Mac Low's original procedural and thematic conception of 1962, and open to all that might come along over the next three decades, the Light Poems are, indeed, a genre all their own—a genre of one, but a genre nonetheless.

It was the combined efforts of Clayton Eshleman and Jerome Rothenberg that brought the first set of Light Poems to publication in 1968. Although the earliest installments were published in journals such *Pogamoggan*, *Joglars*, *East Side Review*, *Dream Sheet*, and *Caterpillar*, it was Eshleman, the editor of the latter, who encouraged Mac Low to contact John Martin at Black Sparrow Press about the possibility of publishing the poems as a group. Rothenberg, who saw the 14th Light Poem published in his journal *Poems from the Floating World* in 1963, encouraged Martin to get in touch with Mac Low. The result was the publication of *22 Light Poems*, after Martin did make contact in February, 1968. Mac Low was more than pleased at the prospect. On the back of an invitation to a Valentine's Day reading at St. Mark's, Mac Low wrote to Eshleman "Martin of Black Sparrow's interested in the Light Poems (whole series)"; by March the initial twenty were in Martin's hands. At that point, Mac Low had no idea what the long itinerary of the light chart might be. Indeed, in his correspondence with Martin, as Black Sparrow Press approached publication of the volume, he makes clear that he'd imagined the 20th Light Poem to be his last. Regarding the bulk of unanticipated material that suddenly appeared in July, 1968, Mac Low wrote to Martin, "What happened were two new Light Poems, one for you & one for the Antins, that forced themselves into existence while I was typing the note on methods."

And that, indeed, is much the way of it. For the next twenty years thirty-eight more Light Poems "forced themselves into existence." Occasionally readers were lucky enough to encounter them, but many went unpublished. They were often performed, and a few superb recordings are extant, in particular his performance of the 36th and 42nd Light Poems while reading with Peter Orlovsky at Naropa in 1975. Mac Low continued to inscribe his Light Poems in his notebooks, once in a while composing them directly by typewriter, losing track of some, discouraged by others, revising selectively. But even some of those that he elected to publish never emerged as planned. The 42nd Light Poem for Paul Goodman, however brilliant it might be, was rejected by both *Poetry* and *The Vir-*

ginia Quarterly Review. Perhaps the centerpiece of the newly published poems, the 29th Light Poem for Olson was on the verge of publication in George Quasha's *Stony Brook* when the magazine met its premature demise in 1970. Mac Low then also promised it to Clayton Eshhleman for publication in *Caterpillar*, which also, sadly, did not survive. The two most significant collections of Mac Low's work—his *Representative Works* of 1986 and *Thing of Beauty* edited by Anne Tardos in 2008—contain some of the finest examples of Mac Low's Light Poems. Here, however, they appear in their entirety (or as near to it as we can currently achieve) for the first time and they are, in all their brilliance, a shining arc-light of their own.

=====

This is my opportunity to thank Anne for the tremendous and trusting invitation to share in the editing of these poems and for her insight, talent, patience, and collaborative spirit I am grateful. Anne's husband Michael Byron offered important advice, support, and editorial input that is much appreciated. Jerome Rothenberg has championed the project from the outset, and I thank Jerry and Diane for their hospitality and friendship. Charles Alexander came along at the perfect moment: fortuitously proposing this volume at the same moment Anne and I first met in New York City. What a privilege it is to work with such a celebrated poet and publisher. The librarians and staff at UC San Diego's Mandeville Special Collections (especially Lynda Claassen and Robert Melton), NYU's Fales Library, Columbia's Butler Library, and UC Berkeley's Bancroft Library have all provided invaluable support. I am particularly grateful to the ongoing support of the staff in my home library, Bruce Peel Special Collections at the University of Alberta, which houses all of the materials related to the first ninety-four publications of the Black Sparrow Press, and who first brought that archive to my attention many years ago. Keisha Armand assisted in the preparation of the manuscript, and I'm fortunate to have worked with her before she moves on to the great things that she will no doubt accomplish. My thanks also to the Faculty of Arts, University of Alberta, for supporting my research.

Finally, my thanks to my partner and colleague Cecily Devereux: whose kindnesses and brilliance have meant so much to me during the completion of this volume, and who in the ongoing poem of our lives shares with me her heart, her home, her love, and, indeed, her light.

— Michael O'Driscoll

1st Light Poem: For Iris—10 June 1962

The light of a student-lamp
sapphire light
shimmer
the light of a smoking-lamp

Light from the Magellanic Clouds
the light of a Nernst lamp
the light of a naphtha-lamp
light from meteorites

Evanescent light
ether
the light of an electric lamp
extra light

Citrine light
kineographic light
the light of a Kitson lamp
kindly light

Ice light
irradiation
ignition
altar light

The light of a spotlight
a sunbeam
sunrise
solar light

Mustard-oil light
maroon light
the light of a magnesium flare
light from a meteor

Evanescent light
ether
light from an electric lamp
an extra light

Light from a student-lamp
sapphire light
a shimmer
smoking-lamp light

Ordinary light
orgone lumination
light from a lamp burning olive oil
opal light

Actinism
atom-bomb light
the light of an alcohol lamp
the light of a lamp burning anda-oil

2nd Light Poem: For Diane Wakoski—10 June 1962

I.

Old light & owl-light
may be opal light
in the small
orifice
where old light
& the will-o'-the-wisp
make no announcement of waning
light

but with direct directions
& the winking light of the will-o'-the-wisp's accoutrements
& lilac light
a delightful phenomenon
a delightful phenomenon of lucence & lucidity needing no announcement
even of lilac light
my present activities may be seen in the old light of my accoutrements
as a project in owl-light.

II.

A bulky, space-suited figure
from the whole cloth of my present activities
with a taste for mythology in opal light
& such a *manner*

in the old light from some being outside

as if this being's old light cd have brought such a manner
to a bulky, space-suited figure
from the whole world of my present activities
at this time
when my grief gives owl-light
only
not an opal light
& not a very old light

neither

old light nor owl-light
makes it have such a manner about it
tho opal light & old light & marsh light & moonlight
& that of the whole world
to which the light of meteors is marsh light
all light it
no it's
an emerald light
in the light from the eyes that are making it whole from the whole cloth
with no announcement this time.

III.

What is extra light?
A delightful phenomenon.
A delightful phenomenon having no announcement?
No more than the emerald light has.
Is that the will-o'-the-wisp?
No, it's the waning light of my grief.
Is it a winking light?
No more than it is the will-o'-the-wisp.
Is it old light?
The oldest in the whole world.
Why do you speak in such a manner?
I suppose, because of the owl-light.
Is it a kind of opal light?
No, I said it was old light.
Is it a cold light?
More like a chemical light with the usual accoutrements.
Like the carmine light produced by my present activities?
More of a cold light than that.
Like what might fall on a bulky, space-suited figure?
Well, it's neither red light nor reflected light.
Are you making this up out of the whole cloth?
No, I'm trying to give you direct directions.
For avoiding a bulky, space-suited figure?
No, for getting light from a rhodochrosite.

Note: A rhodochrosite is a vitreous rose-red or variously colored gem-stone having a hardness of 4.5 & a density of 3.8 & consisting of manganous carbonate ($MnCO_3$) crystallized in the rhombohedral system.

IV.

This time I'm going to talk about red light.
First of all, it's not very much like emerald light.
Nevertheless, there's still some of it in Pittsburgh.
It adds to the light from eyes an extra light.
This is also true of emerald light.
But red light better suits those with a taste for mythology.
As reflected light it is often paler than the light from a rhodochrosite.
Such a red light might fall on a bulky, space-suited figure.
In just such a manner might this being be illuminated during a time gambol.

3rd Light Poem: For Spencer Holst, Beate Wheeler, & Sebastian Holst
—12 June 1962

Owl-light in a tree house [1", 2", 3", or 4" of silence]
singing by the light of a Nernst lamp
porcupines in arclight
see the porcupines in arclight
wait   [12", 24", 36", 48", or 60" of silence]
are there mustard-seed-oil lamps burning in the Persian section of Brooklyn?
I'm inclined to think so.
Anda-oil lamps must light the Andaman Islanders.
Do they give a ruby light?
Aladdin lamps give a light as white as night inside out.

Lamplight on footgear
weathering
aurora light in summer
the dawn light is circumstantial
disregard the neon flush of yesterday
I'd hunt it out if Altoona were Allentown or Muhlenberg LaSalle
Treat it as a question of footprints in snowlight in Cleveland or a diamond in starlight
        Milwaukee comes to mind
incessant spring scintillations.

        [long silence]

Patriarchal light from ancient candles.

        [short silence]

Collect soapstone lamps to light the ice tables a bit in Holstenborg to help Boy Holst
        finish his Greenland story where "they" were
"lit a bit by the soapstone lamps on the ice tables."

A yellow smoky light?
A corrosive light?
A candid light?
A flattering light?
Light given off by a rhodochrosite if a rhodochrosite gives off light.
Enter a chorus of grumbling priests carrying magnesium flares & hoes.

Treat it as a question of data here on the coast & in the light of that data construct
          imaginary parallels to light geometry & paraphernalia for pranks in autumn.

Who burns walnut-oil in lamps?
I see its light as a rich brown light like an over-varnished Rembrandt.
One wd have to have a flashlight to find things.

4th Light Poem: For La Monte Young—14 June 1952

Ordinary light
but neat

a clean north window on a clear morning

IT
TAKES
A
VERY
LONG
TIME
TO
GET
TO
NOON

30

5th Light Poem and 2nd Piece for George Brecht to Perform tho Others May Also Unless He Doesn't Want Them to—13 June 1962

George Brecht
in a white light
sits on a white
wooden chair.

He wears a
white tee shirt
white cotton trousers
white socks &
white tennis
shoes.

He throws white roses
From a white vase
into a white waste-
basket placed
at a challenging distance from the chair.

Around & between
George's chair
& the wastebasket
he has placed
sources of some kinds of light
& emblems of the possibility of others.

He continues throwing the roses into the wastebasket
until he misses.

Then he goes to the rose on the floor
& carefully draws a line on the
floor with
white chalk
from the bottom of the rose's stem
to the petals &
prolongs the line until he hits
or nears
a light source or emblem.

After pocketing the chalk
he retrieves the roses from the wastebasket
counts them out loud
& returns them & the one from the floor
to the vase.

He goes back to the white chair.

As he sits
the lights go out
for as many time-units
of his own choosing
as there had been roses
in the
waste-
basket.

Then George produces a light by means of the source
if the rose pointed to a light source
& if it pointed to an emblem
he makes the kind of light the emblem symbolizes visible.

This kind of light remains visible
for as many time-units
(either ones the same as those that measured the darkness
or different ones than those that measured the darkness)
as there had been roses in the wastebasket.

Among the kinds of light that might be seen now
might be
arc-light
watch-light light
jump-spark igniter light
Aufklärung
lightning
rays of light
cold light
moonlight
naphtha-lamp light
noontide light
luminiferousness

almandite light
enameling-lamp light
a nimbus
meteor light
Jack-o'-lantern light
water lights
jack-light light
refracted light
altar light
Corona-cluster light
magic lantern light
ice-sky light
clear grey light
iridescence
natural light
infra-red light
Reichsanstalt's lamplight
exploding-starlight
Saturn light
Earthlight
actinism
sodium-vapor lamplight
cloud light
Coma-cluster light
alcohol lamplight
luster
light of day &/or
lamplight.

One of these kind of light might be seen now
or
some other kind of light.

After a short darkness
the white light goes on again
& George
on his white wooden chair
throws the white roses into the white wastebasket
until
he
misses.

Then he does what he does again
then more darkness
then
the kind of light
pointed to
by the rose on the floor
then
more
darkness
then George in a white light throwing roses
& so on
until he feels it beautiful to stop.

6th Light Poem: For Carol Bergé—14 June 1962

Carol Bergé in luminosity.
Carol Bergé in bus light trying to see out & read & sleep.
Carol Bergé in amber light.
Carol Bergé in gaslight in a tight dress.
Carol Bergé in artificial light.
Carol Bergé by the light of big guns firing.
Carol Bergé in camphor-oil lamplight.
Carol Bergé by owl-light.
Carol Bergé in the light of a bicycle lamp on a deserted highway.
Carol Bergé in the light of the beach lights at Coney Island.
Carol Bergé in ghost light flickering.
Carol Bergé in the light of a gasoline lamp.
Carol Bergé in a rainbow.
Carol Bergé in garden light at night with long black gloves on up to her bare shoulders.
Carol Bergé in the light of the beacon on top of the Palmolive Building in Chicago which
    is called the Lindbergh Beacon.
Carol Bergé in an evanescent light & then vanishing.
Carol Bergé in the midst of the *Aufklärung* in Weimar bored with Goethe's talk but
    digging his bed style.
Carol Bergé bathed in lambent flame.
Carol Bergé in colored light under a Christmas tree.
Carol Bergé peeing in a gutter by the light of a garbage truck.
Carol Bergé by Earthlight.
Carol Bergé in the *Aufklärung* again learning Persian & writing poems with a quill pen on
    parchment Schiller brought her.
Carol Bergé in amber light smoking a cigarette in a long amber holder & drinking amber
    whisky as she reads *Forever Amber* wincing slightly.
Carol Bergé in gaslight in Reading Gaol sneaking a note in to Wilde from one of his boy
    friends while visiting him disguised as a Salvation Army major.
Carol Bergé in radiance.

7th Light Poem: For John Cage—17 June 1962

Put off an important decision
         in mechanical-lamp light.
Success in a new project will bring lumination.
An exchange of courtesy in the zodiacal
      light reminds you that expenses can
      run high when you insist on light
            from almandites.
For almandites are iron-alumina garnets
      $Fe_3Al_2(SiO_4)_3$.
When of a fine deep red or purplish red,
      from India,
                  and transparent,
                        they are
               "precious garnets."
A lucrative job available in amber light
   does not jeopardize your credit,
                              but
         melon-oil lamplight
                     might.
Your intuitions lead you right
      in cineographic light.
Say what you really think.
The lamp I have clamped to the kitchen
                        table beside the
         notebook I am writing this in
                        gives a sort
         of a student-lamp light although
         it is not a student lamp but
               a PENETRAY.
In chrome light and in light from
   alexandrites,
            spinach-
                  green
               chrysoberyls,
               columbine-
                     red
                  by artificial
   light,

36

from Ceylon and the Ural
Mountains,
money from a
surprising source
belies the belief that there's
always
nothing but
futility in romantic wishes
arising in old light.
Those wishes,
that first arose
in old
light,
light
trailing from
spiral nebulae
and galaxies so distant
that a stone
thrown
at a reading lamp's
light
at a
distance of
two miles
wd be
an unintentional slight
to natural law
compared to the folly
of launching
"space ships" toward them,
those
wishes that arose before
the light of the annealing-lamp
on which your dentist heated foil
made you begin to
avoid taking chances
by
taking chances,
might
make you take a
trip to a scenic region

where
the light's
maroon.
Beware light from a Cooper-Hewitt lamp,
light
derived
from passing an electric current
through
mercury-vapor

light
bluish-
white,
ghost-light from toothbrushes
along the absent 'L,'
beware
the new light on the Bowery,
that promises a
good possibility of money loss.
The receipt of an important invitation
to radiation
's
a secret
not to be discussed
even in olive-oil lamplight,
even in the
extra light of your
elation over the good news,
lead as it might to a
temporary setback
as
the light
waned.
Revenue yielding ideas arise(s)
in orange light
but an exquisite object stirs joy
even in the light of

Reichsanstalt's lamp,

a modified form of

Hefner's lamp,
       a photometric lamp burning amylacetate.
Can an emerald light bring nothing but
      disturbing rumors
                about money?
Orange light yields revenue yielding ideas
     of
       disturbance
   and   recklessness
amidst an uncanny refulgence
    as of marsh light
     or will-of-the-wisp, those
    sparks of cold light
       which sometimes seem to
   follow instructions exactly
         as if they
     were light from kinetographs,
      or fishermen's jack lights,
     but emerald light
        alternating with
     red light & lilac light,
all incandescent lamplight,
      made
     by following instructions exactly
            some
              times
  awaken spectrums
   like the aurora's
     or
    those of
       remembered napalm flames.

8th Light Poem: For Dick & Alison Higgins to perform sometime:
1st Light Play—17 June 1962

Dick and Alison Higgins appear riding a
                    horse in owl-light.

    They dismount from the horse and threaten
            to mount a tandem bicycle that
        is standing nearby either on its own
            stand   or in a bike rack
                            but instead
            they drag the bike sideways to one
                            side
                        sit on the ground
                    beside the wheels
            one on either side of the bike
            & proceed to improvise on the spokes
                            of the wheels
            & to a lesser extent than on the spokes
                on the frame & other parts of the bike.

    Now the light begins to change from owl-light
            to eye light
                    an unexpected assignment
                & as the lights change
        Dick gives to Alison
                    or Alison gives to Dick
                    an unexpected assignment
                to plan a foolish purchase
                                        &
        if they discuss buying an alcohol lamp
                        or alcohol &c
            they shd be lighted by flaming alcohol
                                        &
        if they discuss buying a reading-lamp
                    or books to read
                    or a   series of readings
                    say, at the YMHA, &c
            they shd be lighted by reading lamps
                                        &
        if they discuss buying a Cooper-Hewitt lamp

that is,
  a mercury-vapor lamp,
    or an apartment or loft on
Third Avenue (now lighted by C-H toothbrushes)
  or anything else on that or any other
    avenue or street lighted by
     mercury-vapor lamps,
           say,
tickets to the series of lectures on Wilhelm Reich's
theories delivered in a building on the Bowery
that is part of Cooper Union
tho not the old building where Lincoln spoke
& Dick's & La Monte's & Richard's pieces
  were played
      Dick likes it a lot
         that his pieces were played
       in the hall where Lincoln spoke
      & that's an amiable trait
         one for which we like Dick
  even tho it merely means
  he has a sense of history
      Dick has more of a sense of history
than anyone this side of John Cage
  unless it be La Monte Young
  who's at least as much concerned with it
         now
if they discuss buying something on a
        mercury-vapor-lit
    street or avenue,
       like tickets for
        the Reich lecture
         series
   which Diane Wakowski *did* buy,
    they will be lighted by mercury-vapor
      lamp light,
       &
if they discuss having their pictures taken
or buying Milk of Magnesia
or tickets to a first-night performance
or anything else which might be
  an excuse for setting off magnesium

                    flares
        such as newspapers carrying
                    news that K & K have
    agreed to disarm at once
                    offered
                    immediate UN member-
        ship to China
        which has accepted

    & also agreed to disarm
                        &c
                        &
    if they discuss buying electric bulbs
                electric lamps
            shades for electric lamps
            prisms for electric lamps
            cords for electric lamps
        switches for electric lamps
                    or tickets for
        some activity especially
        dependent on electric lamps
                such as movies or plays
        they shd be lighted by electric lamplight   &
    if they discuss buying a watch
        they shd be lit by watch-light light.
                                Watch out!

9th Light Poem: For the Algerians—27 March 1968

In June 1962 I began & abandoned the first "9th Light Poem: for the Algerians."

Their Light Poem is their Revolution.

10th Light Poem: 2nd one for Iris—19 June–2 July 1962

A useless plan proposed in acetylene light
to a cheery visitor
who carries a lamp that burns castanha-oil
lit
adding its castanha-oil
light
to the acetylene
scene
advancing ignition
of
the refusal of a loan
despite long working hours
stretching to the aurora
& an exchange of possessions
in winestones-oil
lamplight
or a need for stressing modernization
&/ or exploding starlight
are merely petty annoyances
but ether lamp light
threatens
an improvement of conditions
despite
a useless plan
proposed
in acetylene light
& failing in
ghost light.

11th Light Poem: For Richard Maxfield—17 July–8 August 1962

The reflected light of an incandescent lamp
is a kind of illumination.
Certainly.
And the light of an ether lamp
also
but dangerous.
Certainly.
Witness the Parisian movie disaster
after which Montesquiou
(Charlus)
(des Esseintes)
is said to
have pried the charred clothes
from his wife's
corpse
with a walking-stick
to identify it
without
touching it.
Those rays
from a lamp that first made shadows live
& then
exploding
made the living shadows
prevented public acceptance of movies
many years.
The public was afraid.
Why not?
How cd they have know that *any* light
even comet light
(magnified or otherwise made strong enough)
wd do
(if bright enough)
to make the moving-picture-people move?
How cd they have known
these shades
these shades of shade
wd live
in any strong light?

In earthlight even?
Even in earthlight if the earthlight be
intense
& focused thru the film
& focused by a lens in front of the film
to fall upon a screen
with all those image-people & their furniture & pets
& flowers & farms & boats
in focus.
But why are you talking
(asks an imaginary
Richard Maxfield)
in a light poem for me
about the movies?
Or is that the work of chance?
2 chances.
A chance operation
involving numbers & letters
gave me
"ether lamplight"
& the chance borrowing of a book
from Joe & Suzie Byrd:
The Banquet Years
by Roger Shattuck
who told of that terrible fire at the fair.
What fair?
A Parisian society fair.
The Bazar de la Charité
of 1897
"held in a rambling wood-&-canvas structure
off the Champs Elysées"
where the ladies
"set aside a room for a showing
of Louis & Auguste
Lumière's
recently perfected *ciné-
matographe,* which had
rendered obsolete
Edison's unwieldy kinetoscope only
a few months after the latter
came into
use.

46

The film program at the Bazar
attracted many children, and
a turnstile was installed
to keep them orderly.
An
ether lamp
provided light for projection ..."

12th Light Poem: For Julian Beck—8 August 1962

Here comes a letter from a dear friend
written in light unfiltered thru an achroite
(a stone of *some* kind
I dont know anymore
if I ever did
I doubt I did
what it is).

I try to keep informed
about work matters
in that room of colored lights
where friends become
worthy
assets.

I encourage
progressive
ideas there,
but everyone wd rather have
Japanese lantern light
if they said what they really thought.

But light is light,
tho it is
not so certain
that man is *ever* man,
& especially
one feels this after an evening
of argument & turmoil.

Some people have
a watch-bird
watching them
but you
have a watch-*light*.

What emotional ex-
asper-
ation brought about the

finding of
orgone lumination?

Jacinth light
Jac in th light
had a
big
broken
heart
thru which the
sheen
penetrated
while others
post*pone*d
major expenditures.

What's that got to do
with Alexandrite light?

Even if I knew I wdnt tell you.
Why?
Avoid asking for too much light.

That
sounds like
the worst
bigoted
casuistical
Jesuitical
Ro-
man
Că-
Că-
Că-
Că-
tho- [ah] ⎯⎯⎯⎯⎯⎯⎯⎯⎯⎯⎯⎯⎯⎯⎯⎯⎯⎯
[ah] ⎯⎯⎯⎯⎯⎯⎯⎯⎯⎯⎯⎯⎯⎯⎯⎯⎯⎯⎯
[ah] ⎯⎯⎯⎯⎯⎯⎯⎯⎯⎯⎯⎯⎯⎯⎯⎯⎯⎯⎯
[ah] ⎯⎯⎯⎯⎯⎯⎯⎯⎯⎯⎯⎯⎯⎯⎯⎯⎯⎯⎯
lic- [s] ⎯⎯⎯⎯⎯⎯⎯⎯⎯⎯⎯⎯⎯⎯⎯⎯⎯
[s] ⎯⎯⎯⎯⎯⎯⎯⎯⎯⎯⎯⎯⎯⎯⎯⎯⎯⎯⎯⎯

[s] _____
[s] _____
[s] _____
_____ ism.

It isnt.
What isnt?
I wish you wdnt make me tell.
Why not?
It doesnt help the general strike for peace.
What peace?
The peace
between
all the different beasts
(people too?)
(people)!
(too!)
in Hicks's
Peaceable
Kingdom.

The peace
we
or someone
or something
or not
will have in the peaceful society.

What peaceful society?
(Prensky asked
after too many sleepless nights)
when was there ever a *peaceful*
SOCIETY?!
                        SOCIETY IS WAR!
Then, said Julian Beck, I'm antisocial.
(I mean, a real imaginary Julian Beck.)
If society *is* war
we're up
I'm afraid
Shit
Creek

in a leaden canoe
lighted by a nitro-filled lamp of course.
Why a nitro-filled lamp,
Miss
Monroe? I've forgotten.

Perhaps you cd light
the theater
by candlelight
for rehearsals at least
or by
some other innocuous
(what do you mean
innocuous?) means.

What *means* this means?

What,
asked Daniel de Leon,
means this light?
I mean, . . .
What?
O well!

There must be some kind of chemical light.

What?

For photographs of flat roofs & flatter asses.
Who shd flatter asses?
They dont *have* to be flattered theyre great!
Flat asses? No.
No?
No. The rounder the better.
I thought
'rounders' were - - -
Shut up!

You wdnt say
that to me in
*lil*ac light!

You *bet* I wd!
Even if we were attending a public *event*?
All events are public.
What a thought! Where . . . ?
I didn't get it from *anyone*; I *bled* it.

In a white earthlight?
Hell no; in
car-
    bide-
        lamp-
            light — .
You mean from acetylene? Well . . . . .
thats what a *car*bide lamp burns
but
that
aint
LEgal!
        Nonsense!
Neither is nonsense.
I'd rather have . . .
If you say "h———————" . . . .
I won't.

I'll just turn on the electric-arc-lamp
& start the movie.
The movie of your life?
The movie of your life.

13th Light Poem: For Judith Malina—9 August 1962

Is it possible to have ogres & vampires for friends? asked the baby gargoyle?
Yes child hush the dawn light is coming.
The cocks are crowing in their improvised cages in the top floor window of the tenement
                    across & down the street,
the tenement once a chic Jewish apartment building
in this densely Puerto Rican & dark American street.

The sweat pours from me for I havent slept & I hate the friends I love & fear &
light cd pour from me instead
if I were Vinoba Bhave
or Martin Buber
or Ramana Maharshi
or Sohaku Ogata or —

I'm not.

14th Light Poem: For Frances Witlin—10 August 1962

Even among those high-minded people of the *Aufklärung*
neighbor slandered neighbor
reproaching each other all day
mad against each other
sworn against each other
& the light of that 'enlightenment'
was blood-color
tho transmitted thru no carnelian.

Time was wasted that way then
& time *will* be wasted
but with all the benefits that might come
thru an executive
who might take time for calm reflection
& by taking
time for
calm
reflection
might
allow us to take
time for calm reflection
I'm afraid that calm reflection
wd be merely a 'brown study'
for we're mere sards
transmitting blood light
reflecting brown light.

Now we share the work & benefits
such as they are
of what we have
even tho we often feel
we're made to appear in a foolish light
by what we do.

An innocent light?

The innocence of fools
or the foolishness of innocence?

Transmitted thru glass or ice cut to a prism
ice light
is iridescent light.

An irrelevant light?

All light is relevant to each light
& each light to every light
& each light to each light
& every light to each light
& all light to every light
& every light to all light
& each light to all light
& all light to all light.

Is that lucid?

Yes.

It is all about light.

Mere secondary phenomena of luminiferous ether.

Light!

Light.

If you follow instructions exactly.
at noonday
in the noon-light
the experiment may prove disappointing
but what cd be clearer?

A nimbus.

So you are seeking sainthood!
Who said that?
A silly fool.
An uninnocent fool.
A foolish foolish fool.

A foul fool.

A melodramatic fool.

A posturing self-lacerating fool.
A self-destroying fool.
An exhibitionistic Dostoyevskyan fool.
An ordinary fool.
An ordinary thief of property.
A proper fool.

A sneaky fool
patting himself on the back
for being and admitting himself to be
a fool & a liar & a thief.

A *light*-fingered fool?

A fool who knows a fool may have to compromise
& foolishly uncompromising
compromises most
when foolishly it seems to him he's least *un*compromising.

Radiance!

That's your name for what we call mere radioactivity.
Deadly.

Deadly radiance.

A spectrum of shade.

Like long working hours leading to fatigue & nothing more.
Nothing more?
O Frances do not break your heart!
do not break!
Break
nothing more
nothing
more
nothing.

The tall light trails thru the sparrow chirps
& glass tinkles
swept
in the area below these stranger windows
as in the Bronx I know
by Evelyn the dark resentful super
altho no beer cans
dance across concrete
with high hollow clatter
impelled by dark resentment & a broom.

Tĭ-dĕl, tie-dáhr, tee-dĕn, tuh-dăn, tuh-dŏom.

Make no promises.

I've made one promise only.
One promise.
One promise only
made itself me.

But what it means is
what it means.

Only two know this.
Perhaps
one more
who sits to my left
smiling
or glum
or glumly smiling
or grimly smiling
or grimly
glum.

Boomelay boomelay boomelay boom.

Together weeping for his lost dark splendor
hating what he made of us
& what he allowed
what he thought we were
all of us
make of him.

How we sat together gritting our teeth.

Was it true?
Or another lie to make the fancy leap?
To show the know we were in
together.

She who makes no promises she cannot keep.
Or if she does
makes the limit of each promise clear.

Not you my dear.
I did not mean to speak of *you* here.
I find I have.

The traitorous light turns'
as the
whirling earth
turns.
The traitorous light turns from pale
blue
to grey.

My traitorous heart turns from one to the other loyally.
Faithfully my traitorous heart
turns
trying to make no promises or none it cannot keep
or none that cannot keep it
or none that cannot keep it keeping them.

What can I say?

Say the waxing light
depends upon no purchase of electrical equipment.
Say
a distant matter is delayed
a distant matter
a lambency
leaping about us
not yet.

Say nothing.

The light of a lamp burning winestones-oil
is preferable by far
altho I've never seen it
to one that threatens us
with danger
from chemicals.

My lucky number?

491
tells me to forget
a previous worry.

A *previous* worry?

What did I see before in a worrisome light
that I see in such a light
no longer?

Is it merely morning movie light
oh one four
that tells us to expect a change for the better?

Time will be wasted
but honesty
whether in light from an Argand lamp
or arc-light
or *Aufklärung*
is
the best
policy?

Tragedy.

Idiocy.

Honesty?

An aureola springs around a formerly hated form.

You must stay alive.

15th Light Poem: For Susan Witlin—11 August 1962

'In the middle of the road of our life'
the attention advances & ignites
the balance
& the intuitive light
alive in any baby
                    not mere lucence
        of places
                    & plants

16th Light Poem: For Armand Schwerner—22 August 1962

In what light
do you read a poem
you wish to demolish?

An unsympathetic light.

In what light
do you wish to appear
when you read a poem
with the intention of demolishing it?

A superior light.

In what light
do you wish to appear to be reading a poem
when you read it
with the intention
of demolishing it?

A critical light.

In what light
do you appear
to one who tho suffering
from an ugly reading
of a poem with the intention of demolishing it
sees that this reading
arises from a suffering of the one
who reads it
with the intention of
demolishing it?

An 'insecure' light.

What has caused the suffering
our nearly-modern jargon tags
as 'insecurity'
in the one
—in you—

who read my poem with the intention
of demolition?

I am glad to say
that I can throw no light on this.

But may not this reading
have arisen from a genuine desire
to reprimand an error
that is
by exposing the poem
in an 'objective' light
& subjecting
the poet—that is to say, me—
to a kind of friendly, more or less, sadism
a little rougher (but poets can take that—
(—& anyway a poet who prints in such a place
(shd be ready
(for worse than that, I suppose)
than the kind the squares
—the other squares, that is,
—the ones you
don't want to seem like & unlike, etc.—
call 'kidding'—
to aid your friend &—
(I hesitate to add for you now—
(& anyway the word seems to stink—
("fellow-poet")
fellow poet
by your corrective light?

A long question
& one a little darkened by
all those parentheses
but one the light of friendship—
let me be precise:
the light of acquaintanceship beginning to deepen to friendship
despite
—o well—is the word 'setbacks'?—can illumine,
a long
question

to be answered in the light of beginning friendship
with 'Yes.'

Is this an attempt to see
you
—this critical poet-acquaintance who is
slowly,
with 'setbacks,'
beginning to be or seeming to begin to be
my friend—in an
affirmative light?

Yes.

Then why do I speak of your
reading the poem in an
'unsympathetic light'
in order to demolish it in order
that you might appear in a
'superior light'
& appear to be reading the poem
in a 'critical light'
& why do I mention seeing you
(as you read the poem that way to demolish it)
in jargon light
in semi-or-pseudo-scientific-
semi-or-pseudo-psychological light: in
an 'insecure' light
—that is—
—I see I'm in the midst of another long question—that's all right—
why do I try to throw the light of ridicule
& the light of questionable-motivation-finding &
other unfriendly lights
on this simple act
that I can
see in this affirmative light
as merely your attempt to throw
the light of your critical insight
on this 'bad try' of mine
at showing a superior trait of some of my neighbors
in the objective & admiring light

I think it deserves?

Is that the end of the question?

I think so.

Because I think the act was more than double.

You mean
you prefer to see it in a complex light?

I mean that I prefer
to see it as I saw it in the light of those
strange
sleepy-making lamps in
Jerry & Diane's
living-room, I mean
I saw a light of hatred
begin to fill your eyes as
you read Ed's
magazine & that
you began to read my poem as a bad example
of what was in it
& then saw, or seemed to see, who wrote it,
& then
went thru with it anyway as you saw
that the poem aroused your dislike
just as much or
possibly more because you thought I shd know better
& that
what the poem said
aroused your dislike
as much or more than how I said it
—because it was clear
that I said it as simply as possible
in order to state a simple
admiring group of observations—
& that *this*
(in the light of retrospect this seems
(certain) was what
aroused your dislike,

that is, you possibly
disliked that I thought these things
& certainly disliked that
I felt them worth writing a poem about
& even more, that I
felt it right to publish such a poem,
or *any* poem,
in such a magazine, (I, for
(several reasons difficult to convey
(to anyone outside the
(—I guess you call it 'world'—of
(pacificists, anarchists,
(pacifists, Catholics,
(peaceniks, crackpots, &
(admirable young souls
(determined not to fall in any slots—
(but willing to risk not
(only their
(lives—find
(editor & magazine confused & confusing &
(full of needless verbal violence, in
(reaction—necessary
(reaction
(against the mealy-mouthed goody-goodies
(full of 'principled' hypocrisy which they
(arent even aware of—who think
(talking like third-rate
(preachers cd
(help to make the governments make peace
(—& thus, I find it
(an admirable enterprise
(directed against all canons of good taste
(& all proprieties—a needful
(grab-bag of all kinds of writing
(much of it necessarily
(bad
(—but in the midst of it all you find,
(as Ed intends,
(some of the best—a different kind of
(enterprise, certainly,
(than the magazines you are proud to publish in)

& this
—now that we're out of parentheses—
is what I thought mistaken,
& thus, that your
reading of my poem in a
way that cd only
make it appear worse than it possible *cd* have been
arose *not* from your
viewing it in the light
of your best critical insight
but from seeing it in the light of
hatred.

Was the hatred aroused
by the magazine's
title (*FUCK YOU,*
A Magazine of the Arts)?

Yes,
at first that & the cover, of course, but
then
not only by the contents
in general but
the contents of this particular poem
aroused your own
—why shd I hesitate
to say it now that I see it?—
—worries over overweight, at
least,
this seems to be a part of it, & possibly
what I mean
(I see it now, only felt it then) by your
being seen in an 'insecure'
light as you
read my poem of admiration for the frank dark girls who love their own voluptuousness
          & show it off with
no thought beside 'the men will want me'—
no thought of good-or-bad-taste
but the taste their bodies give them
for virile bodies—as you
read it woodenly, making it seem,

in the light of understated ridicule, not
even a sensible statement,
much less a poem.

Then what has happened to that 'affirmative' light?

Mixed with the need to continue
because you had begun
revealing the poem in the light of
ridicule, hatred, & so on, was
the genuine wish to
illumine this 'error' by
the light of your critical insight.

Is this making excuses,
trying to see a near-friend
in the best light?

Yes, & besides,
I think that seeing that issue alone
might make the whole enterprise
(can it be called a magazine? it's
(an action of
(complicated revulsion, at
(least that, &
(more than that)
seem different & certainly
worse than it is, & I can
see myself in the light of
memory & imagination
reacting
(had I seen it first
(as you did
(raw & out of all context)
far more violently & unjustly &
besides, you
made me see some words in the poem
need changing.

17th Light Poem: For Paul Williams—27 March 1968

In August 1962 I began & abandoned the first "17th Light Poem: For Paul Williams."

His Light Poem is his light sculptures.

18th Light Poem: For Rochelle Owens—29 October–29 December 1962

I.

I know a silly girl
who has a munificent muse
I don't understand her a bit   but
I understand her muse a little better
(they're hard to put together
& if I call her 'silly'   it's not at all
that I don't like her   really
she's the strangest poet of us all   & we're
a strange bunch   of verbals
but she's   (I mean Rochelle's
just about the strangest

        (now Jack Smith
        (the poet   photographer
        (worshipper of women
        (to the point   where
        (his photographs are poems
        (of woman-centered *eros*
        (where women are mingled
        (with men dressed as women
        (now he's strange too
        (but he & his muse are strange the same way)

(Alas for
(Jack Smith
(his kleptomania's
(got him put in jail
(Oh Jack   Jack
(was all that
(costume jewelry
(worth getting put into
(The Tombs?   What
(now?   [Well, now
([he's out.])

Now I pause
because   the dawn
light   is lightening the top

of the tan kitchen curtain Iris drew on
with green & orange & purple magic markers.

II.

Rochelle, if she were sitting under an
ultra-violet lamp, might laugh
to see how *cer*tain words
change when seen in different lights.

If the words were 'governor,' 'milk,'
& 'love,' how different they might seem
in Subway Light on advertising posters, &,
in Candlelight on photographs made with X-Rays.

For Rochelle, as for us, the problem of Actinic Rays   seldom
arises—more rarely than for most among the TV-watching peoples of the world: East &
            West
we know best, who shun the invisible death rays
from the video tube.

III.

In what light wd Rochelle view
a cucurbit (or cucurbite),
a cuckoo clock, a cuckoopint, and
a cucumber tree?

In a cucumiform light.

In what light wd Rochelle see
a cuckold with a cuckoopint
of 23 cu. cm.
and a cucking stool?

In a cucumiform light.

In what light wd Rochelle look for
a cucurbite?

In a cucurbitaceous light.

In what light wd Rochelle regard
the 41 cu. cm. of Cuchulainn's cucurbite,
his cucumber tree's cucurbite,
his cucumber's cucurbit,
his cucumber's cuckold,
his cuckoo spittle, and
his cuckoo clock?

In a cuculate light.

In what light wd Cuchulainn
(or Cuchullin)
view Rochelle viewing
Cuchullin?

In a cucumiform light
near a cucking stool.

In what light wd Cuchullin
see Rochelle?

In a cuculiform light
filling 94 cu. cm.

In what light wd a cuckold
frothy with cuckoo spittle look for
a cuckooflower, a cuckoo clock, or Cuchullin?

In the light of his own cuckoldry by Cuchulainn.

In what light wd he regard the cuckoo spittle?

In the cuculiform light by which Cuchullin wd regard Rochelle.

19th Light Poem: For Iris—7 February 1963

(breath pauses at line endings)

pillow light pillow heels pillow underwear
light pillow light light light
pillow light pillow heels pillow underwear
heels heels suede ceiling heels
pillow light pillow heels pillow underwear
underwear envelope red under-
wear watersound underwear underwear
underwear tape-
recorder
light light light light light
pillow light pillow heels pillow underwear
light pillow light light light
light light light light light
light light light light light
pillow light pillow heels pillow underwear
light pillow light light light
pillow light pillow heels pillow underwear
heels heels suede ceiling heels
pillow light pillow heels pillow underwear
underwear envelope red under-
wear watersound underwear underwear
under-
wear tape-
recorder
heels ceiling suede ceiling heels
heels ceiling suede ceiling heels
suede suede suede suede suede
ceiling red Iris ceiling ceiling ceiling
ceiling
heels heels suede ceiling heels
pillow light pillow heels pillow underwear
light pillow light light light
pillow light pillow heels pillow underwear
heels heels suede ceiling heels
pillow light pillow heels pillow underwear
underwear envelope red under-
wear watersound underwear underwear

under-
wear tape-
recorder
underwear underwear red under-
wear watersound underwear underwear
under-
wear tape-
recorder
envelope under-
wear envelope under-
wear osculation envelope envelope
envelope
red neck red
underwear underwear red under-
wear watersound
underwear underwear under-
wear tape-
recorder
watersound tape-
recorder watersound green tape-
recorder watersound watersound watersound
watersound tape-
recorder
underwear underwear red under-
wear watersound underwear underwear under-
wear tape-
recorder
underwear underwear red under-
wear watersound underwear underwear under-
wear tape-
recorder
underwear underwear red under-
wear watersound underwear underwear under-
wear tape-
recorder
tape-
recorder tape-
recorder tape-
recorder envelope under-
wear tape-
recorder tape-

recorder tape-
recorder underwear watersound tape-
recorder tape-
recorder
light light dog light light
light light light light
light light light light light
light light light light light
light light light light light
pillow light pillow heels pillow underwear
light pillow light light light
pillow light pillow heels pillow underwear
heels heels suede ceiling heels
pillow light pillow heels pillow underwear
underwear envelope red under-
wear watersound underwear underwear
under-
wear tape-
recorder
light light dog light light
pillow light pillow heels pillow underwear
light pillow light light light
light light dog light light
light light light light light
light light light light light
light light light light light

20th Light Poem: For Bob & Joby Kelly—19 February 1963

I.

One lying revealed in the light of a watching-candle
was last alive in acetylene light.

The light of night lie softly over him.

And the lavender light the old doctor referred to as "flimmering"
the lavender light he saw on the walls of his room-sized accumulator

Doctor—
            Doctor—
poor,
        not-so
                    old
                        man
                            who loved us so
and all God's marvelous magnetic fleshy mechanisms:—
                                                "*not* mechanisms," you wd say
Did you see them at night on the walls of your cell?,

you obstinate German
                            letting them kill you
        as you knew they wd
            you knew your own biopathy
        rather than let 'their' courts rule on a matter
                            of natural science

I see Dr. Wilhelm Reich in a maroon light sadly weeping a benevolent red-faced ghost
        weeping for the crippled children of the poor

I see him in the agate light of what he was convinced he had discovered for mankind &
        how he felt he was being recompensed for having made that discovery why am I
        thinking of Wilhelm Reich?

I am writing this by an electric light.

What do they mean by an 'altar light'?
Is it the light given off by an altar as a whole

or the light given off by some particular kind of candle, say, or lamp on it?
Is it merely the light of an altar candle or an altar's entire light?

Altair's entire light??
The light of the "brightest star in Aquila,
(used in computing lunar distances)"?

Why no
merely the light of a sperm-oil-burning Keats lamp
God protect all sperm-oil-burning Keatsians
and all those worthy Wordsworthians
God forgive John Donne his ghost for having unwittingly put them in the shade!

Did Captain Ahab burn a Keats lamp?
(Someday I shall ascertain whether Ishmael ever told us.)
Not today I'm listening to Beethoven
I-don't-know-what quartet is playing on the radio.

I found a while back that I've got 13 kinds of light in this poem
or rather twelve, with one
(lavender light)
listed twice.

13 means cards in a suit so soon cards will be playing cards will be among the means used.

I have a Florentine pack that Alexandra gave me
a marxist-leninist avant-garde composer *may* have stolen the joker with the big-bare-titted
          jester girl on it.
"This deck is a limited edition.
The miniatures were painted by the French artist Paul-Émile Bécat.
after the famous paintings of the Old Masters,
and the description we have of the masterpieces
destroyed upon order of the Monk Savonarola."

The description is exaggerated but theyre
often somewhat subtly dirty
                              sometimes just
mildly pornographic.

Anyway here it is
or will be in a while but now

who comes wreathed in electric arc light?
Is it Jeanne (or Jeanette) d'Arc,
daughter of Jacques d'Arc of Dorémy not Arc where's Arc?
I always used to wonder where 'Arc' was didn't you?
Well 'd'Arc' was just her last name, it seems.

Nobody wants to say anything about 'Arc'
only '*Arc, Jeanne d'*. Same as JOAN OF ARC.
"*Joan . . . 4. J. of Arc* (1/6 1412–5/30 1431),
" 'The Maid of Or-
" 'leans';
"a French heroine and martyr who compelled the
"English to raise the siege of Orleans;
"was captured;
"burned;
"was beatified
"by Pius X,
"in 1909;
"canonized in 1920;
"in-
"troduced in Shakespeare's *1 Henry VI.*
"5. a country
"wench." O no. Or rather
what were those angelic visitors whispering
to that Joan
of do
  re
   mi
the melodic saint rivalling Cecilia
whom some have called a war-mongering tomboy
but Saint Guillaume Machault
composed the mass for the coronation of her Dauphin
as yet unbeatified uncanonized St. Guillaume Machault
composed it for the doublecrossing liege lord of
Ste. Jeanne d'Arc,
   of Doremy

Some say she was a great magician not a musician
& that she wd have gotten away but they
either were quicker than she was
or she scorned to run away as Socrates had scorned to

for a somewhat different or was it the same reason?
Does Doremy have an accent on the 'e'?

It doesn't have an accent it has an '*m*':
it's Domremy
it's in the Vosges
"*DOMREMY-LA-PUCELLE* [*don*],
"village de
"l'arr. [ondissement]
"de Neufchateau
"(Vosges);
"sur la Meuse;
"c'est
"là que naquit Jeanne d'Arc,
"dont la maison subsiste
"encore;
"['1918 / *tous droits réservés.*]
"273 h.[abitants]
"ch.[emin]
"de f.[er]
"E.[st]"
[de Paris?]

Did you ever read a science fiction story
that was supposed to be happening
on a planet of a star in
one of the Magellanic Clouds?

"You choose it because it fits
"the chronological exigencies . . .
"Mozart's Post-Horn Concerto"

"Julius Baker Flute
"Sylvia Marlowe Harpsichord
"Händel's Sonata in A Minor"
[Mozart later]
Noble melancholy Händel
may he sing forever in the heavenly choirs.

A St. Germain lamp is a student lamp
   "see STUDENT"

so I saw "*stu'dent,* . . .

"—*stu'dent-lamp*

"n.[oun]

"A lamp having an Argand burner . . .

"["A burner producing a hollow

"["cylindrical flame,

"["supplied with air within as well as with-

"["out;

"["by extension,

"["a gas-

"["burner in which this principle is

"["used."]

"supplied with oil by

"gravity from a separate reservoir

"connected with it by a

"lateral tube,

"the whole being usually adjustable in height."

"A Juggernaut

"covered with rose-petals

"rolling benignly downhill . . .

"Mozart's

"Post-Horn Concerto No. 9 . . .

"K. 520(?)"

II.

So now the dirty Florentines help to decide things.

Wd it be on a planet of Altair

or on ordinary Pluto solar vagrant

that a maroon light wd prevail

even at high noon?

Today is Tuesday 19 February 1963

at 6:39:57 A.M., E.S.T.

It's later now.

Mozart's 9th Post-Horn

                              (is that like Post-Impressionist?)
Concerto
that has a Köchel listing of course that *may* be 520—

Who was Köchel?
Old conscientious countin' Köchel?
standin' in the lamplit nightlight countin' Mozart

and from the agate ring on his forefinger flashes
the light of an altar lamp
& the lavender light of a
watching-
candle.

Köchel on a planet of a Magellanic Cloud star
countin' the Mozart goin' by
in a Magellanic Cloud's
star's
planet's
light
unaugmented by acetylene . . .

No he sits with Schubert spectacles on
at a little table with a St. Germain
lamp
("A lamp having an Argand burner ["&c."]
("supplied with oil by
("gravity from a separate reservoir
("connected with it by a
("lateral tube,
("the whole
("being
("usually
("adjustable
("in
("   height." [?]) on it.

There's probably someone living there in the
Magellanic Clouds—How
cd there be all that light
& no

life?

But can you imagine poor Köchel living in
perpetually maroon light
or lavender light
or agate-filtered light
itself a nearly
maroon light but more jewel-
like?

Aha sad lone cross-
fluting male
joker,
Did Keats
ever
write by the light of a Keats lamp?

"airborn . . .
"a defective air-
"foil . . .
"isn't *that* a piece of music? . . .
"Köchel 320
"The post-
"horn . . .
"Mozart my obsession after the news what *more* can we ask . . . of our advertisers
         . . . proud . . .
". . . uncompromising attitude . . .
". . . reach the kind of people
"suited to their product . . .
"This is Bill Watson
"listening with you
"WNCN . . .
"15,000 watts . . .
"WNCN incorporated,
"a subsidiary of . . . incorporated . . .
"New York City."

"Almighty God,"
the next man's gonna say. . . .

He did.

"as we begin this broadcast day . . .
"especially the blessing of music . . .
"with its unending power to console
". . . fear . . .
"and ignorance . . .
"amen. . . . "

Why's Machiavelli shown on the Jack of Spades
with a bare-assed maid, one side up—
the other way up he's admonishing I think
a fully-clothed maid
he's making her give back something
shaking his forefinger
his other forefinger
at her
as he holds out his left hand for what he's making her give back.

"awed by music"

"Mozart . . .
" 'a piece of music which wd make the pianist sweat.' "

"K. 299 . . . Flute & Harp"
Mozart hated flutes & harps they say
"C Major"

Mozart in the light of an electric arc
accompanying a silver flute
upon a silver harp.

The electric arc light is warmed
by being reflected
from the bared breasts
of the female
'lover of Verona'
who's smelling a flower with her blouse on,
t'other side up.
She's also taking something from her boy-friend's hand
she wears pearls
and some sort of locket or pendant that
nestles between her

proud-
shown
breasts.

The electric light is yellow in the kitchen
Mozart's flute & harp turn golden & glow
as a "rip-tooth of the sky's acetylene"
forebears as yet to conflict with the
nearly-altar light
of this golden lampshade we found on
a street in Greenwich Village in the winter
after
we'd taken some of Iris's
paintings to a gallery in a
Stanford White building on 5th Avenue.

It's nothing but shaded electric light
but it is truly golden now.

What has it to do with the light of a watching-candle?

"A candle used at a wake
"or at a watch with a corpse."

No more than the light from an electric arc might.

Even if that electric arc were on an altar & its only light?

Perhaps Father Mapple's sermon was delivered
in the light of a Keats lamp.

But "we can subvert with pop records,"
says Bill Watson
playing Köchel 191, a
Bassoon Concerto.
He's erected an electric-arc-lit altar to Mozart there in the Concert Network,
not a Keats-lamplit one,
or one lit by
the agate-refracted lavender light
of a St. Germain lamp
(as Köchel's no doubt was).

Well no, not a lavender light
and more likely reflected from
than refracted by or thru
agate.

I mean Köchel's was probably not lavender
or even maroon light—
—the light of Köchel-who-knew-a-good-thing-when-he-saw-it-
or-rather-heard-it-
(I mean when you're gonna spend your life countin' stuff
(you want to be sure you've chosen something to count
(there's plenty of—
(like Mozart)'s
St.
Germain
lamp.

The nightlight is gone.
The daylight is here.
It's 7:58:17 A.M.

It's seconds later now.
55 seconds now.

Can you imagine your brothers in the Magellanic Clouds?
If they are sinners Christ died to save them too.
Cd they be free of Adam's guilt—
or rather, how cd they *not*?

Three bare 'adventuresses'
toss money
tender pearls
& pick up coins:—
in a watching-
candle's
light?

It's one of Cézanne's clear
gray
days.

A bare blonde & brunette
drape red-leaved vines
over a large red
heart
on swirling blue drapery
edged in gold and red
in an
"Allegory of Love"—
in the
light of a watching-candle?

The light of a Keats lamp
burning sperm oil in the midst of the
light of night.

If there were an
acetylene lamp giving
lavender light
wd that lavender light be
a brighter light than nightlight
or lavender electric light?

Is the light of a good St. Germain lamp
as bright as that of electric light?

& cd a Keats lamp's light be brighter
than an acetylene lamp's?

What light wd you have on *your* altar?

III.

Random combinations & permutations
& permutations of combinations
of a 13-member set
of names of kinds of light
(2 members of which are alike)
drawn, by means of playing cards
& RAND random digits,
from a 280-member set
of names of kinds of light

(no 2 of which are alike)
of which the initial letters of the names
are solely the letters found in the names
Iris Lezak & Jackson Mac Low
& of which the names
are set forth on a chart
constructed by modification of a photo-offset form
entitled "EDITORIAL DEPARTMENT PAYROLL DISTRIBUTION"
& used (or formerly used) by
the accounting department
of Funk & Wagnalls Company
& discarded with countless other things
when they moved from 153 East 24th Street, New York 10,
to 360 Lexington Avenue, New York 17,
just before the end
in February 1962 (I think)
of my four or five-month job
as a temporary "assistant editor"
of *THE NEW INTERNATIONAL 1962 NEW YEAR BOOK*
A COMPENDIUM OF THE WORLD'S PROGRESS
FOR THE YEAR 1961
a job Paul Blackburn the poet got me into
when I needed it
as badly as I need one now
& he was a seemingly permanent
"associate editor"
while lovely Drenka Willen mildly ruled
as editor (but then she quit
in the middle of the book
to save her health
& Ginny Carew ruled the roost
before & after *my* job's end
& when the book was finished fired Paul).

IV.

So there was this St. Germain lamp
perched on a Magellanic Cloud
or rather, paling the tiny-enough-here light of the latter,
adding its bit to the nightlight,

It's Haydn *Hoch der Kaiser*.

I don't even remember there being a maroon
light at the
University of Chicago & if not *there*—
—*where*?

Some electric light is
lavender light in the light of the night.

What causes a lavender light?

& what wd or cd cause a maroon light?

& what do you or we mean by 'an agate
light'?

What by 'mar-
oon light'?

Do you like electric light?

I like electric-arc-lamp-light.

What do you like about electric-arc-lamp-
light?

That it's neither a lavender nor an
agate-reflected or -refracted
light.

Is it usual to find lavender altar lights?

No but even less usual is light from agate lamps
distilling Magellanic-Cloud-light
falling
from nebulae & clusters seemingly
part of the Milky Way
but really
many faraway galaxies & clusters.

Have you ever had an 'aggie'
& let the light fall thru it
—say, thru a lavender 'aggie'
or a maroon one
—have you ever let *only* the light
from the Magellanic Clouds fall thru it?

As written by hand this is the top of page 21 of Light Poem 20: to the Kellys.

Watching-
candles
stand at the edge of the nightlight
while a St. Germain lamp
may sometime
serve
(& undoubtedly one *has*)
as a watching-candle.

Is there such a thing as an
electric St. Germain lamp?
Or an electric-arc-lit St.
Germain lamp or an
acetylene-illuminated one?

Lavender light is lavender light in the
night
light
unaugmented by acetylene.

In the nightlight the Keats lamps were flaring
in place of watching-candles.

And where watching-candles were replaced by electric-arc-lights
or by ordinary altar lights
with
or without
auxiliary Keats lamps, . . .

Maroon and lavender light
comes from a St. Germain lamp.—
that

St.
Germain lamp!

Is acetylene light
whiter than any
electric light?

Can altar light be acetylene-lamp-light
& where?

In British West Africa?

On what kind of nights
with what kinds of light
do they use Keats lamps for light?

The light from altars lit with sperm-oil-burning Keats lamps
and that from those lit by lavender electric
& maroon-illuminative
lamps.

Have you ever knowingly seen in the bare sky
with the naked eye
the Magellanic Clouds?

What is the Large
Magellanic
Cloud?

It
"is the brighter of the
"two famous clouds of Magel-
"lan.

"It lies outside the
"Galaxy
"at a distance of some 50,000
"parsecs
"(1 parsec equals 19,200,000,000,000 [19 trillion, 200 billion] miles).

"This

"galaxy is chuckablock with
"blue giants,
"supergiants,   and
"glowing clouds of gas.

"The
"very bright patch of nebu-
"losity is known as the Ta-
"rantula Nebula.

"It has been
"estimated that if the Taran-
"tula Nebula were as near to
"us as the Orion Nebula
"(Plate XI)
"it would appear
"as bright as the full
"Moon."

What is the Small Magellanic Cloud?

"Much to the surprise of the as-
"tronomers vast tracts of hy-
"drogen gas have recently
"been discovered in this
"Cloud.

"But there is little dust
"and few giants here.

"Why
"the two Magellanic
"Clouds
"should be so different in their
"stellar populations is an unsolved problem."

Agate altar lamps
can easily overwhelm the light from the
Magellanic Clouds
which
"provide

"some evidence that star-
"formation is a cyclic process that
"includes a dust-
"free phase.

"The Large
"Cloud contains dust,
"gas,
"and extremely luminous blue giants.

"The
"Small
"Cloud
"contains gas but no dust,
"while the few blue giants in the
"Small
"Cloud are not nearly so bright as those of the
"Large
"Cloud.

"This would suggest that the cyclic process in the
"Small
"Cloud is now at the phase
"in which the dust
"of the last star-
"forming period has been evaporated
"or blown clear away.

"The
"Large
"Cloud seems on the other hand to be at just the oppo-
"site phase,
"with plenty of dust,
"condensed gas,
"and with very
"bright blue giants.

"It is possible that a few million years hence
"the situation will have been reversed,
"with the
"Small

"Cloud then
"containing the condensed gas and very
"bright stars,
"and with
"the
"Large
"Cloud going through a dust-
"free era."

I think we used to have bulbs in the
tassel-shaded lamp by the piano
& the dark-red-was-it?-vase-lamp
that gave a nearly maroon
electric light.

Was the base of the lamp of dark agate?

Some of those 1920's & '30's bulbs also gave
lavender light.

I've seldom been at night in acetylene
light
but I remember the smell of calcium carbide in water turning into acetylene for light
but I've never seen a Keats lamp or its light,
as far as I know.

& I've never seen
I don't think I've ever seen an
electric-arc-lamp-lit altar.

& I've never seen watching-candles
unless those
Jewish candles in glasses cd be
the last shrunken commercial epigones
of watching-
candles.

I've never seen a Keats lamp
being used in place of a watching-candle.

Is acetylene light brighter

than Keats-lamp-light?

Only at night?

When is acetylene light lavender?

When is it lavender?
When the light from every
St.
Germain
lamp is.

On what night is the light from every
St.
Germain lamp lavender?

The night when the light from every
Keats lamp and electric-
arc-
lamp
is.

Have you ever really seen an altar light of agate?
No I haven't.
Nor have I seen many giving a really
lavender light.
Or a maroon one.

21st Light Poem: For John Martin—30 June 1968

While typing a note
for the book of my Light Poems John
Martin's about to publish,
I'm moved to write one more,
for
as I copy the chart I used
in writing most of the others,
I see many kinds of light
that never appeared in any of them.

Jacinth light isn't one of them:

Hyacinth,
the gem.

In mod-
ern use
jacinth
an hyacinth
are sometimes distinguished
jacinth being used of a gem more
nearly pure orange
in color.

or

of the color jacinthe

A color,
red-
yellow in hue,
of high saturation and high
brilliance.

or

Tawny.

A tawny or orange or red-yellow light—
hyacinth light:

A precious stone of the ancients,
of a blue
color,
perhaps
the sapphire.

A plant
fabled in classic myth
to have sprung
from
the blood
of the youth
Hyacinthus
a beautiful
Laconian
youth,
beloved
by Apollo

by some supposed to be
the Turk's-
cap lily
Lilium
martagon,
by others the iris,
larkspur,
or gladiolus:—
used only as transliterating or
representing the Greek
or Latin
word.

Commonly,
a
well-
known
plant of the genus
Hyacinthus,
having
spikes
of bell-

shaped
white,
pink,
yellow,
or purple
flowers;
also,
the bulb
or flower
of the plant.

See
Hyacinthus.

A beautiful
youth beloved by Apollo
and
killed by the latter through
an unlucky throw
of
the discus
(or,
according to another version,
by
Zephirus,
out of

jeal-
ousy).

From
his blood
Apollo caused the hyacinth
(see
Hyacinth)

A plant
fabled
in classic
myth to have sprung from
the blood of the youth

Hyacinthus
by some supposed to be
the Turk's-cap lily
Lilium martagon,
by others,
the iris,
larkspur,
or gladiolus.

to spring
up,
with
the exclamation of woe,
Ai,
marked on its petals.

Like Adonis,
he doubtless
per-
sonifies vegetation,
scorched and killed by the summer sun.

The cult of Hyacinthus in Laconia
dates
from
prehistoric
times;
but
his association with Apollo is
probably
of late
origin.

Cf. Hyacinthia.

A summer three days' festival
in honor of Hyacinthus and Apollo.

It was one of the most
important
festivals of the Peloponnesus,

its chief
center
being Amyclae
(Hyacinthus
being
the son
of the Spartan
king
Amyclas).

The festival began
with mourning
for the
death of Hyacinthus
and ended with rejoicings for his re-
birth.

See APOLLO,
1;

One of the most important
of the Olympian
gods,
especially conspicuous as the god of manly youth
and
beauty,
of poetry and music,
and of the wisdom of oracles.

In his primitive
character
he was the fosterer of herds
and
flocks,
guardian of youth,
leader of colonies,
and protector
of the village
and its streets;
he was
perhaps

also a god
of
vegetation,
esp(escially) in the Peloponnesus.
where
he was associ-
ated with Hyacinthus,
a part of the *Hyacinthia* being con-
secrated to him.

The Athenian
harvest
and expiation festi-
val of *Thargelia*
was also
his.

At Delphi,
where he was
the
chief god of the oracle

(cf. DIONYSUS)

An Olympian god,
originally
a god
of vegetation;
later,
god
and giver
of the grape and its wine,
in which character he
was worshiped
with orgiastic rites
and conceived as leader of a wild rout of satyrs,
maenads,
and sileni.

He was also patron of the drama.

A later
name of Dionysus,
which came to be the usual one among
the Romans

(cf.
however,
Liber),

An ancient
Italian
god of fructification
(per(haps) orig(inally) Jupiter Liber)
and,
after
his identification
with Bacchus,
of the grape.

A goddess
Lib´era
(Lib´ĕrȧ)

(see Ceres)

Goddess of
the growing vegeta-
tion.

In her oldest
worship
she was
closely associated
with the earth god-
dess,
Tellus Mater,
her feast,
the *Ce´´ri-*
a´liȧ
(sē´´rĭ-ā´lĭ-ȧ),
was celebrated on

April 19,
honoring
the young
vegeta-
tion.

In response to
the Sibylline oracle,
about 500 B.C.,
the
Greek cult of Deme-
ter,
Dionysus,
and
Kore was introduced
into Rome,
Demeter
being identified with
Ceres
Dionysus
and
Kore
with Liber
and
Libera.

To this cult
belonged
the later
worship
of Ceres
as
a corn and earth
goddess.

Ceres is the daughter of Ops and Saturn.
was associated
with him

Their festival,
the *Lib´´er-a´lia*

(-ā´lĭ-à),
was on March *17*.

is *Bacchus.*

To it
cor-
responds
Iacchus,
by which
he was hailed
at the Eleu-
sinian mysteries

(which see),

the most famous
of the religious
mysteries
of
the ancient world.

They originated at Eleusis,
probably
under Cretan influence,
in prehistoric times,
and after
the
conquest of Eleusis
by Athens
were made a part of the
Athenian state religion,
though rites remained in charge
of the Eumolpides
and Keryces
ancient families
of Eleusis.

They were celebrated yearly
in historic times.

The *Lesser
Mysteries,*
held at Agrae,
a suburb of Athens,
in Atheste-
rion
(Feb(ruary)-March)
were concerned
with legends of Diony-
sus and Kore
(Persephone)
and were probably devoted to
a purification of candidates
for the *Greater Mysteries,*
held in Boedromion
(Sept(ember)-Oct(ober)).

These
began
on
the
13th,
with the departure
from Athens
of the ephebi,
who on
the next day returned from Eleusis
with
the sacra.

The
15th to the 19th
were occupied with ceremonies
which
in-
cluded the *halade mystai*,
("to the sea,
mystae")
at which
the candidates bathed in the sea.

On the 19th
and 20th
occurred the great procession to Eleusis,
the latter day
being known
as *Iacchus*,
from the cry raised by the
marchers who bore
an image of this god
(Bacchus,
or Di-
onysus).

The initiation proper
occurred between the 20th
and 23rd,
and comprised purifications,
fasts,
and the wit-
nessing
of rites or sacred dramas
portraying
the legend
of
Demeter
and Kore.

To initiates
of the second degree,
the
epoptae,
as distinguished from the *mystae,*
was probably
reserved the representation
of the sacred
marriage
(of Zeus
and Demeter).

Initiation was believed
to ensure

happiness
in the future world,
and
perhaps
included the imparting
of formulas
to be used by the soul on its passage thither.

Cf. ORPHIC MYSTERIES

The secret rites and doctrines of the
adherents of the
interpretation of Dionysiac worship
as-
cribed
to Orpheus
as founder.

The rites included cere-
monies of great antiquity
and probably savage origin,
such
as a sacramental feast of raw flesh,
putatively the body of
Dionysus
under the form of Zagreus

(which see);

A god
of possibly
Thracian origin,
identified
with Dionysus
and worshiped in
mysteries
which included
the eating of the flesh of a bull.

The influence of this worship
reappears

in Orphism.

they also
included the more
civilized
symbolism
characteristic of the
Eleusinian mystery
(see under ELEUSINIAN,
adj(ective)).

Their
essential import was to teach
that the initiate
might
by pure
life
and asceticism
achieve
that mystic identification
with the
divine
nature which the Dionysiacs sought
in orgiastic ec-
stacy
and hence might attain
immortality.

They also
(pos-
sibly through Egyptian influence;

cf. BOOK OF THE DEAD)

A collection
of formulas,
prayers,
and hymns,
knowledge of which was believed to
enable the soul in its journey
into Amenti

(which see)

The region of the dead,
a
subterranean realm
whither the sun descends.

The soul
entering Amenti
was conducted by Anubis into the hall
of
Osiris,
was judged by the 42 judges,
and either
passed
thence
to Aaru
or was consigned to torment.

The *four*
genii of Amenti
were children of Horus,
usually repre-
sented upon the four canopic jars.

The four
were the
man-
headed
Amseti,
associated with the south,
the dog-
headed
Hapi,
with the north,
the ape-
headed
Duamutef,
with the east,
and the hawk-
headed

Kebhsenuf,
with the
west.

to
pass successfully
the foes
set to impede its progress,
to call
upon the helpful gods,
and to answer
properly
the 42 asses-
sors,
or judges,
in the hall of Osiris.

Its authorship
was
spread through many centuries.

Copies of it,
or of some
of its chapters
were buried with the mummy or inscribed
on the sarcophagus
or tomb.

Cf. Pyramid Texts.

Inscriptions found on the walls
of five
pyramid tombs of the Old Kingdom.

They are the
earliest form of what
later became
the *Book of the Dead.*

purported to give instructions
for conduct of the soul in the

world
below.

some of the formulae are preserved in eight
Orphic tablets,
inscribed plates of gold found in the graves
of believers,
seven in Italy,
one in Crete.

where he was also known as
Eleutherios.

Bromios is
a poetic title.

The epithet
Liknites refers
to his child-
hood;
the name *Dithyram-*
bos
is derived
from a choral
ritual in his honor.

He was
also
identified with the bull
god
Zagreus,
a tree god,
Dendrites,
and the wild
Thracian deity
Sabazios,
while as the Cretan *Lenae-*
us he was
the inventor of vine
culture
as well as the civilizer of

the world.

His chief festi-
vals in Attica were
the *Dio-
nysia*

(which see)

Any of the festivals held in
honor of Dionysus;
often,
specif(ically),
the Dionysia of Attica,
in
connection with which
Greek drama developed.

This latter
comprised
the *Rural Dionysia,*
held in autumn,
where the drama is said to have originated,
and the *Great,*
or *City,*
Dionysia
held in the spring,
at which plays
were
regularly given from the time of Pisistratus.

See BACCHANALIA,
1;

A festival of Bacchus
celebrated
by the Romans
with orgiastic rites.

cf. CHORUS.
1;

In Greek drama,
a company of singers
or
chanters.

In the developed
tragedy it occupied a role
fluc-
tutating
between
that of participants in,
and interpreters of,
the action.

The earliest chorus was a group of singers
under a leader
who sang
the dithyramb at the Dionysia.

In 534 B.C.
Thespis introduced
an actor
who held a dialogue
with the leader
of the chorus.

Aeschylus introduced
a sec-
ond actor,
and Sophocles
a third.

The chorus,
however,
was still an organic element of the drama,
the choral ode
forming a running
commentary on the play.

TRAGEDY.

A
literary composition,
esp(ecially) a narrative,
which excites pity
or terror
by a succession of sorrowful events,
miseries,
or
misfortunes,
leading to a catastrophe.

Go,
litel book,
go litel myn *tragedie.*

Chaucer.

A dramatic composition
depicting a serious story,
in
which,
typically,
the leading character is
by some passion
or limitation
brought to a catastrophe;
also,
generically,
drama of this type,
or the composing
or acting of it.

Greek
tragedy
is severely
simple in plot and incident.

The dialogue
is in verse
and is interspersed
with choral odes.

The action
as a whole
is conceived as a manifestation
of fate,
in which
the characters are somewhat
passively involved.

Modern
tragedy is typically complex
and varied in plot,
and
at the
present day
is more characteristically in prose.

The action
is conceived as the free working out
of the individual char-
acters.
See CATHARSIS,
2;

Purification
or purgation
of the emotions
by
art;—
a variously
interpreted term
used by Aristotle in his
description of the effect
of tragedy as
"through pity and
fear
effecting a *catharsis* of these emotions."

In English
usage it has acquired two leading senses:

a Elimination

or
moderation
of
emotional disturbances,
esp(ecially) those caused by
pity
or fear,
through stirring up,
and providing an outlet
for,
these feelings
by means of artistic
(esp(ecially) tragic)
repre-
sentation;
hence,
a mood of emotional release
and
intel-
lectual serenity
induced by art.
b Purification of the emo-
tions,
esp(ecially) pity and fear,
by cleansing them of that which is
selfish,
morbid,
irrational,
etc.,
through inducing
imagina-
tive
participation in
the sufferings of others
artistically
presented,
esp(ecially) in tragedy;
hence,
a mood in which the feel-
ings excited are refined,
exalted,
and universalized

by being
given an impersonal
or ideal
direction by art.

22nd Light Poem: For David Antin & Eleanor & Blaise Antin—1 July 1968

Can the light of a dark lantern cause
word division?

Not when artificial light
enforces complementary distribution.

But in a vivid light
an adverb
may function as a call.

Wd that require a kind of incandescence?

Not in daylight.

Wd anda-oil suffice?

If the lamp were new enough.

But what might be the effect
of nova light?

It would be a modifier.

Wd it modify a word?

Perhaps a noun.

Wd a tantalum lamp do more?

More than an ignis fatuus wd.

Wd it ensure close juncture?

Noonlight wd do that better.

What about early light?

Its lucence might provide

a kind of punctuation.

Better than electric light?

Better than an azure exit light.

But what wd make for rising terminal juncture?

Only the light of noontide.

Then what wd opalescent light provide?

Rising terminal juncture.

In what focal area?

Any one
that might be reached
by rays of light.

Even if only by those
of a Berzelius lamp?

Even a transition area
lit by lightning.

Cd a verb be made inactive
by the aurora australis?

If falling terminal juncture intervened.

If light fell thru an iolite
bluely
what might it originate
by analogy?

Nothing in a nonlinguistic context.

Not even an ignis fatuus in starlight?

Not even a new verb.

Is light from an electric lamp
enough to do that?

Not even enough
for a novel noun-determiner.

What about an annealing lamp?

That sets my teeth on edge.

What about a night light?

That might.

Comparatively speaking?

That depends on the kind of word.

Wd a tungsten lamp do better?

If it cd affect articulation.

That needs illucidation.

Do it with a verb-phrase.

Cdnt I do it with a nova?

No, sir.

23rd Light Poem: 7th Poem for Larry Eigner—15 January 1969

In a lavender light
roadways are where they are,
altho far above them
an aurora borealis
streams at the end of a process.

That refulgence is what it is
in all those positions
far above the houses:
it has no aims
but is drawn to junction
like a firefly in a field.

Now the light is red in the night,
but far below it
the yellow grass
seems to give off
a yellow light of its own.

But an emerald light's approaching dance,
procession of innumerable protons,
threatens to disperse the old colors
as the aurora bends & twists thru the precipitous atmosphere.

In the kitchen where all these lights are imagined
incandescent-lamp light streams at midday,
yellow despite the poem's green aurora.

When a switch is clicked,
the natural light,
whiter and bluer tho reflected from bricks,
makes one look up
to the bricks at the top of the wall at the edge of the roof:
stained yellow against a deep blue sky by the midday sun.

Looking down at the chart
one gathers a dreadful vision
of earthlight on the devastated greenish-brown gray surface of the moon:
—who'd want to trade?

Let them carry freight in those ships,
moon minerals scooped by machines
resistant to the ruthless rays,
not men or other sentient beings
dear to the fathomless Buddha.

24th Light Poem: *In Memoriam* John Coltrane—19–26 January 1969

Why this cinematographic light?

For some poems.

What poems?
What no.?
What MAPS?

Mostly poetry in an orange light.

Let's hope just not a magazine
in lavender light?

Quite right.

In the tall clear light of the "I,"
a friend,
Toby Olson,
showed me
a rose
light.

An artificial light?

No,
Magellanic Cloud light.

Not ether-lamp light?

Neither
that nor
chandelier
light.

Nor any other old or old-time light?

Nor any other old or old-time light.

How can the howling void
be cheated of his light?

Probably not
by meteorite
light.

& almost certainly not
by candelabra light
or oil-gas light
or any other halfway human
light.

What about natural light?

Not quite.

This
very
cineographic light?

Yes,
but mixed
with camphor-oil light
& aquamarine light
& lantern
light.

Why has the light been taken away?

Why has his light been taken away?

He is now his own reflected light.

An aureole?

No, more like light from a nitro-filled lamp.

Of which
other than its name
I know nothing.

But Lord! how the light of the eye illuminates all of the visible world!

A Juicy Fruit light

             An office light

A hospital light

             A nervous light

A Compōz light

             An "on" light

A low-cost light

             A temporary light

A reading light

             Attention light

No light

             An east light

    (subway light)

III.

If there were to be a joke about light,
what kind of joke ought it be?

Ought it be a hot joke
or ought it not be negative?

& what if it ought to be cool?

What wd it mean to be obliged to be
cool?

Ludicrous.

But most true jokes are cool,
if not, as a rule,
cruel.

Ancient jokes
aren't necessarily better.

An ancient joke about light,
a necessary joke about light,

an everlasting joke about light:

> "& The Lord said:
> 'Let there be light!'
> & there was light."

IV.

Wdnt he want us to think of him in a joyous light?

Obliged
to be joyous
by burdens of joyous memory!

Or memory surround us
with an obliging light,
a peculiarly
hallowed
light.

Or is it merely the missing sunlight
of the night that is his absence?

It is the cool light
of the luminary organs of night—
moon,
planets,
stars,
clusters,
nebulae,
galaxies—
all the universe beyond the sun as luminance.

One can imagine him standing
in the ordinary light
of a terrestrial night.

But can one imagine him really standing there
in the real light

of any real night?

One can only imagine him
as if he were standing
in the ordinary light of a terrestrial night:
—one can only imagine him in an "as-if" light.

The truth is the negation
of that imagination:
—a negative image on
an emulsion sensitive to negative light.

An emulsified light?

An earthly light,
one hardly disturbed by the waves of sound
reflecting from his absent presence.

V.

In what kind of light
does he journey at this time?

In a consolidating light
or otherwise;
in whatever light falls upon him.

Is he still in the concluding light?

No, he is not.

Is the light reluctant?

See the fifth line of this section.

But there the light is not determined!

Already you see the light!

Already one sees the relaxation of the light.

Diligently pursued,
light's reluctance,
like Philomel into nightingale,
turns into its relaxation.

Does this yield a sensation?
Is it known by sensation?
Affected by sensation?
Itself a sensation?

Is it a lessening of sensation?
A loosening of sensation?
A lapsing of sensation?
A lack of sensation?

A distance.

VI.

This is a song for John Coltrane
who sang unending psalms.

Tho the grooves of his records
like the visible Trane
come to an end,
he sang unending psalms.

He sings unending psalms.

VII.

CHÊN!
the hexagram of thunder & orgone
—twice the trigram of thunder & orgone!

CHÊN!
the hexagram of movement
—twice the trigram of movement

CHÊN!
sprouting, quickening thunder
—twice sprouting, quickening thunder!

KU:
the hexagram of decay:
—wind at the base of a mountain

KU:
wood under the hard,
—the bland under the obstinate, mild under perverse.

Other words:
if
we directly serve the will of heaven;

by doing so
we act as sages who may safely do
whatever they feel is worth doing.

FU:
The hexagram of return,
of successful return.

FU:
thunder & orgone, movement, sprouting & quickening,
deep in the womb of the earth.

They return whence they
came,
spending seven days in all upon their coming and returning.

COMMENTARY ON THE TEXT
This hexagram presages success
because the firm returns

(to the bottom of the hexagram
from which it
was absent in the previous hexagrams) .

Movement and willingness to
move
(the trigram K'un,

earth,
often symbolizes willingness,
glad acceptance)
are conjoined;
this explains why going forth and coming in
entail no harm.

The next three sentences
imply that this activity is in
accord with the movements of heaven.

It is in
the return cycles that the very heart of the working of heaven and
earth becomes apparent.

For it is only when the whole series is completed
that we can understand
the reasons for many things

(death,
winter
and so on)

which,
at the time,
seemed unpro-

ductive,
negative
or positively evil.

merchants were unable to travel.
Even the rulers abstained from
touring their territories at those times.

Ultimately a great
defeat takes place.

Disaster

is about to overtake the ruler
and for at
least ten years there can be no hope of putting things to right.

VIII.

A gentle light or the light of gentleness.
A component light or a light with many components.
An exhausting light or the light of exhaustion.
A reward-bringing light or one for which a reward is brought.

A changing light or the light of change.
The light right now or the light appearing now.
The light below us or the light that reaches us here below.
A certain light or the light of certainty.

The trigram of light or the light from a trigram.
An approaching light or the light of approach.
A conjoined light or the light of conjoining.
A responsive light or the light of response.

IX.

the fork truck
                    (fork lift)
the electric tractor

the air outlet valve;
the diving helmet
                    (diver's helmet) :

the schooner yacht 'America'
                              [1851]
the start

the transom;
the pepper plant:

the well deck

the funnel capping
                    (*Am.* smoke stack cap)
the whip aerial;

the snowball;
the ear tab
the edge

the asymptotes
                [a and b];
the base,

            a circular plane
the line or horizontal line oscillator
the centering magnet

the anti-distortion
                        (equalizing)
                                    magnets

the screening
                (shielding)
the purple border;

the pearl diadem
the short doublet
the slashed doublet

woman of Nuremberg
                    [about 1500]:
the goalkeeper

treading water;
the five-metre
                (*Am.* meter)
                            platform
                (stage,
                    board)
the meadow

(lawn)
                        for sunbathing or
lying in the fresh air
the turn umpire
a competitor touching the side

the franking value
the newspaper packet,
                        printed

matter
            (*Am.* printings)
                        at reduced

rate
            (*Am.* second-class matter)
                                    in

the newspaper wrapper
the charity surtax;
                    the nominal value

                                    (face
                        value) :

the fitting marks

                    (aligning marks,
                            Am.
alining marks)

the lithographic stone
                        (calcareous
slate stone,

            Am. shale) :
the printing forme
                    (printing form)

the drawing handle
                    (crank)

the covering ground

                        (asphalt ground)
the leather roller
the sponge for moistening the litho-

graphic stone
the colour print
                    (*Am.* color print;

chromolithographic print)
the litho crayon
                (litho chalk) ,

                            a crayon;

the one-side print
the printer

the pressure regulator
the copperplate press:
the cardboard

                    (pasteboard)
                            distance
                                    piece

the fine sieve
the cotton disk or disc
the loading shelf

the instrument panel
                            (gauges for
temperature and pressure,

                    Am.
gages) ;
        the transilluminating and

checking instrument
the washed-bottle extractor

the cream-cheese machine

X.

John Coltrane stands in jewel light in a park
near a fountain rim
by a wall
as a school mistress
(nobody's governess,
merely a schoolma'am)
passes amidst orgone radiation.

Then a swan in half-light,
startled by a Salvation Army soldier
(as who has not been startled by some salvationist or other?)
beats his wings on the water
gleaming in the natural light of his frightened whiteness.

But when a female Salvation Army cadet approaches,
securely ensconced in a clear cold light,
John Coltrane jumps into a goldfish pond
which immediately flimmers
with orgone lumination.

Into this visible lucence
a horseman,
a rider,
a man out riding,
a fellow out for a ride,
someone out riding,
some rider,
some horseman
                        (one of the horsemen
splashes.

The nearby swan
awkwardly flaps his half-clipped wings as,
half swimming,
half flying,
he speedily makes his getaway.

The bonnet of the female Salvation Army cadet
lies on the gravelly pavement between the two ponds.

John Coltrane is no more to be seen.

When I said that he stood in jewel light
in a park,
that was a fantasy.

When I said that he jumped
into a goldfish pond
which immediately flimmered
with orgone lumination,
that
was a fantasy.

Imagine a park:
a fountain's empty basin
in a truant light:
an amateur photographer
comes to take a picture,
setting up an artificial light
that drowns out the night light
& the northern lights
that rise behind the plane
that soon bathes all in napalm flames
that contribute but a mite
to earthlight.

25th Light Poem: For Iris Lezak—26 January–4 October 1969

I.

Look:
that
is a sleeper-layer:
it lays sleepers.

Now
look at it in ice light:
that's right;
now try ruby light.

Now look at this ballast-roller:
does it ever roll ballast?!—
wow!—
just don't take its picture by igniter light.

That's a steel sleeper
glimmering in sodium-vapor light
—can a sleeper-layer
lay steel sleepers?

Do rail bottoms rest as well
on steel as on wooden or concrete sleepers?
—by what form of luminescence
may the rail foot's rest be measured?

II.

Is the light of 2:30 AM "early light"?

What wd prevent its being seen in this way?

New considerations.

Ones involving an inner check rail?

That sounds too much like Irving Babbitt & Paul Elmer More.

The rail web rests firmly on rail foot.

Do passing trains' wheels strike sparks?

Only when the wait sign comes on.

That sounds too much like Irving Babbitt & Paul Elmer More.

No, they were more like frogs.

Devices made of rail sections so constructed & assembled as to permit
        the wheels on one rail of a track to cross another rail of
        an intervening track?

No, frogs----*you*know----frogs.

III.

"Actinism" was once the name
of the science of the radiation of heat & light.

That's obsolete now.

Now "actinism" means
the property of radiant energy
(found especially in
shorter wave lengths of the spectrum)
by which chemical
changes are produced,
as in light-sensitive photographic
emulsions.

& actinic rays are
any of the rays possessing actinism,
as the
green,
blue,
& ultraviolet rays of the spectrum,
which
have a marked photochemical effect.

Does the light of a Kitson lamp
contain actinic rays?

IV.

Over a slide chair
(over a slide plate)
each heel blade of a frog
is eased by an invisible mechanism.

The sole plate screws
(the base plate screws)
keep the other rail feet resting
firmly on the sleepers.

What light can you throw
on the invisible mechanism
that eases the frog over
in time to avert a wreck?

& what of the spring washer
that the nut keeps firm
against one side of each rail fish-plate or joint bar
while the bolt's head holds the other against the rail web?

At the end of this poem
a rushing railroad light
falters . . .
& smashes for lack of a spring
washer.

26th Light Poem: A Light Poem for Elspeth—8 October 1969,
September 1975, & 29 November 1977

Emerald Light.

Since we met again by chance,
there'll be no more chance than that in this,
unless the restless ocean of the mind
be as random & as regular in its motions as the sea
tossing up its jetsam on the beach.

Lilac light.

Summer & lilacs in full bloom,
evening & the stars shine clearly over the deserted garden,
the mellow southern breeze,
disturbing the tallest trees,
makes probable & usual the shaking of the largest lilac bush,
shadowed by a large blue spruce.

Secret light. Starlight.

The sky is so clear
the stars' light alone,
without the light of the mirror of the sun,
illumines the open spaces of the garden & the lawn,
but leaves the swaying lilac bush in shadow.

Pottery light.

The pale light of a pottery lamp,
filled with scented oil,
flickers in the heart of the largest lilac,
swaying to & fro with the leaves & blossoms,

    ever
        falling, tho the lamplight flickers.

Emerald light.

Is this the green of Indiana pot,
or the green of any foliage,
any vegetation
but
mushrooms, & molds,
waxen pale Indian pipes?

Torrid light. (Tailored light.)

Light tailored
by changing the site to the tropics:
the Caribbean . . .
Africa . . . the Amazon . . .
somewhere with luxuriant vegetation
a South Sea isle
unspoiled by visitation
commercial penetration,
exempt from other civilizations'
exploitation.

Hot light?   Yes.

Hot light beats down on a pearly beach:
shell shards . . .
        crystals . . .
            pebbles . . .

sparkle as they scatter it;
sun glistens on moving bodies
perspiring as they cry pleasure:
after last
shudders
they sleep a little in the burning sun
before they creep into shadows of palms beside the beach
to sleep
a little longer.

27th Light Poem: For Jerry (Jerome) Rothenberg (An Essay in Poetics)—
10–11 October 1969, 19 May 1970, & 20 January–25 February 1975

I.

A B C D E F G H I J K L M N O P Q R S T U V W X Y Z
1 2 3 4 5 6 7 8 9 10 11 12 13 14 15 16 17 18 19 20 21 22 23 24 25 26

J–10, E–5, R–18, R–18, Y–25 = "ee" — 2 + 5 = E–7 ;
R–18, O–15, T-20 = K–20, H–8 = S–8, E–5, N–14, B–2 = M–2, E–5,
R–18, G–7

J–10 = JACK-O'LANTERN LIGHT
E–5   = EARTHLIGHT
R–18 = REFRACTED LIGHT
R–18 = REFRACTED LIGHT
Y–25 = E–7 = ETHER-LAMP LIGHT

R–18 = REFRACTED LIGHT
O–15 = AMAZONSTONE LIGHT
T–20 = K–20 = KINDLY LIGHT
H–8   = S–8 = SHADED LIGHT
E–5   = EARTHLIGHT
N–14 = NOONDAY
B–2   = M–2 = MOONLIGHT
E–5   = EARTHLIGHT
R–18 = REFRACTED LIGHT
G–7   = J–7 = JALOUSIE LIGHT

Is it Jack–o'–lantern light
or earthlight—
this light that's refracted over here
    to where I imagine I am—
or is it refracted light
of an ether lamp?

J–10 = JACK-O'LANTERN LIGHT
E–5   = EARTHLIGHT
R–18 = REFRACTED LIGHT
O–15 = AMAZONSTONE LIGHT
M–13 = MOONSHINE
E–5   = EARTHLIGHT

Not Jack-o'-lantern light,
& probably not earthlight,
but light refracted thru
an amazonstone,
bright green amazonstone light,
possibly moon shining thru stone
(possibly earthlight).

How cd we know
whether or not
light refracted
by an amazonstone
is kindly light?

[a long silence]

Here I have a shaded light,
earthlight
or noonday
or moonlight,
but even if it be earthlight,
it is a refracted light
that filters thru imagined jalousies.

II.

Imagined jalousies
can only refract
imaginary light—
imaginary earthlight
or imaginary moonlight
or the imagined light of an imagined noonday
—but can imaginary earthlight
ever be imagined as a shaded light?

& what can make an imagined light
be imagined as kindly,
& who can imagine light
refracted by an amazonstone
who's never seen one?

142

Can one who's never been far from the earth
ever imagine earthlight
as one can imagine moonshine
or even imagine light
refracted by an amazonstone
once one knows it's green?

Can one ever imagine earthlight
as one can imagine the flickering yellow light
(or maybe merely remember it)
of a grinning orange pumpkin Jack-o'-lantern?

I can only imagine ether-lamp light
as a kind of bluish movie light,
a horrible light,
since all I know of it
is from Shattuck's *Banquet Years*

I quoted it in the 11th Light Poem
for poor dear dead Dick Maxfield,
whose light escaped or leaped
before this poem began.

—Let me sing you requiem,
dear Richard, dear friend,
you *are* a great composer,
just as you thought you were,
& your murderous doctors were wrong,
just as you must have known they were,
except at moments like the one that took you away:
peace,
Richard,
peace.—

In 1987 at a charity bazaar in Paris
"in a rambling wood-and-canvas structure off the Champs Élysées"
they "set aside a room for a showing
of Louis and Auguste Lumière's
recently perfected cinématographe . . . .

"The film program attracted many children,

and a turnstile was installed to keep them orderly.

"An ether lamp provided light for projection . . ."

& the whole place burned up.

Tho I've never seen it,
I can imagine the light of an ether lamp
refracted thru water,
but I who've never seen,
directly or reflected or refracted,
true earthlight
can hardly imagine it
as easily as well-remembered Jack-o'-lantern light.

III.

Why talk about Jack-o'-lantern light or earthlight,
refracted of reflected,
& why mention the light, reflected or refracted,
of an ether lamp
when the dog is barking crazily in the yard?

I can remember Jack-o'-lantern light
as easily as I can hear the dog
barking & crying crazily in the yard,
but the crazy sound of her barking in the yard where she's been chained
& stands in the dark in the rain
blots out all possibility
of my imagining earthlight,
refracted or reflected or direct,
or amazonstone light,
direct or reflected or refracted,
for I can barely imagine moonshine
this dark & rainy night
when I hear poor Josie,
whom the landlady owns, not we,
& who's been chained in the yard with the silent new male dog,
barking & crying crazily in the yard
in the dark
in the rain,

& nothing in me wants to make the effort
to imagine
earthlight.

I cannot imagine light
refracted by an amazonstone
while Josie's crazily barking,
& never can I imagine
any light that's kindly
as she's barking, barking crazily in the yard.

I can only imagine
letting Josie loose
in the shaded light of streetlights
that falls on her on the driveway in the yard beside the house;
& rather than half-illusory earthlight,
I can barely imagine
ordinary noonday light or moonlight
as Josie barks & barks in the rainy dark;
& any earthlight imaginable
is sure to be refracted
not by jalousies
but by Josie's crazy barking.

IV.

Even the lamp's electric bulbs
are giving a kind of darkness
as Josie barks in the yard
& I hope against hope
that those in the house next door
will let her loose before I'm forced to do so.

Altho when I open the window
I find the rain has stopped
& the moon & a star or planet
are shining,
I know I'll soon be forced to let her loose
& risk a fight with Rev. Williamson
if Josie keeps on barking crazily
& crying on her chain in the yard in the dark

as the unchanging light of streetlights
barely makes her visible in the yard.

V.

A full orange Jack-o'-lantern moon,
is rising toward the zenith
as Josie sits in the yard
quietly whimpering
—so quietly you often cannot hear her with the windows closed—
but sometimes barking loudly,
usually when people pass by,
walking their own dogs.

A full orange Jack-o'-lantern moon,
shining in the cloudy sky,
nearly at the zenith,
is all that's left of the lights from Jerry's name.

The lamplight of my double-headed aluminum-colored gooseneck lamp
& the greenish reflected streetlights
& rarely passing headlights
are all the light that's here
besides the orange Jack-o'-lantern moon.

But an airplane flashes green & white & yellow light
as Josie starts her barking once again
after "the Rev" and her handyman come in.

I wait to see what "Christian love" will do,
confronted by the crazy
barking & the crying
of Josie in the Jack-o'-lantern moonlight
& the shaded light of streetlights.

What has stopped her barking now?
I can hardly bring myself to look
down from my upper window & across the yard
to see into the shadows
where Josie now seems silent.

The streetlights & the headlights barely glimmer
as I sit in the yellowish lamplight
writing the poem's ending
& wondering if it's whimpering I hear
below the city's roar
& that of passing jets.

Is the high-pitched sound I hear
whimpering or birds
or "merely" in my ears?

Raising the window, I hear her softly crying,
but when she hears the window rise
or sees me looking out,
she begins to bark once more
as crazily as ever.

I should have left
bad enough
alone.

My cowardice because I have no money left to move now
makes me end this poem in disgust,
with aching legs & head & a sore throat,
just before I push the clinky switch
to darken both the double gooseneck's bulbs.

28th Light Poem: For Jill Boskey—11–12 October 1969, 12–14 July 1970

J–16 = Jasper light. Who's that?
        Jasper who?

Jasper,
a green chalcedony or any
other bright-
colored variety,
except carnelian;—
used to
render
L.
iaspis,
Gr.
iaspis.

An opaque,
compact,
uncrystalline variety of quartz,
stained red,
brown,
green,
yellow,
etc.

When green with
red spots it is the bloodstone.

Jasper is mentioned in
Ex.
xxviii.
20 as one of the stones in the breastplate of the high
priest;

in
Rev.
xxi.
18 as the foundation of the wall of the
New
Jerusalem.

It is thought the substance meant was a
dark-
green or opalescent stone.

Jasper ware.

A color,
yellowish-
green in hue,
of low saturation and
very low brilliance.

Cf.
JASPER GREEN,
COLOR.

In textiles,
pepper-
and-
salt
(which see).

Having black and white inter-
mingled in small spots;
hence,
of a dull or neutral gray.

A pepper-
and-
salt cloth or suit.

A pepper-
and-
salt color.

The harbinger-
of-
spring.

I–8 = Inner light.
    ("How cd Emerson rely
        on 'inner light' to get him by?")

It's years since the last meeting of Quakers I ever attended
(it was also the first)
twenty-
six to thirty years ago in
Chicago.

Is it inner light
that makes you more daring & more strong
than I cd ever be?

Is it inner light
that gives
Daddy
Warbucks,
so undeservedly,
such gallant magnanimous foes
as these?

150

May I reverse
our supposedly assigned
roles?

May I admire
your strength and daring
& tremble to be embraced by them?

L–14 = LUMINIFEROUS ETHER

luminiferous
[light-
carrying].

Transmitting,
producing,
or yielding light.

luminiferous ether.

See
ETHER
3.

Physics.

A medium postulated in the undulatory the-
ory of light as pervading all space,
even intra-
atomic
spaces,

and as transmitting transverse waves,
as those of light;
—called specif[ically]
the
luminiferous ether.

The prop-
erties ascribed to it
(extreme tenuity,
absolute continuity,
high rigidity and elasticity,
etc.)
are very remarkable and
its existence is at present denied by many.

According to
Einstein,
the geometrical properties of space render the
hypothesis of the ether unnecessary.

The earth rotates on its
axis and revolves around the sun:
the sun and its en-
tourage revolve around the galactic center.

Where is
the
Galaxy going?

And what can we use as a frame of
reference to find out?

Fifty years ago astronomers thought they had a frame

of reference in the luminiferous ether—
a mysterious
substance pervading the universe—
which was invented
to explain how light traveled across otherwise empty
space.

Experiments produced negative results,
however,
and the ether joined the doctors'
humors and the biol-
ogists'
spontaneous generation of life on the historical
curiosity shelf.

Now,
unexpectedly,
astronomers *do* have something
pervading the universe that they can use as a reference
to measure the earth's
(and the
Galaxy's)
motion.

It
turns out that the universe is filled with very weak
microwave radiation believed to be the residue of the
"big bang"
that created the universe tens of billions of
years ago.

It appears to come from every direction with
equal intensity.

This characteristic,
known as isotropy,
suggested a
new experiment to
Edward
K.
Conklin,
a graduate stu-
dent working under
Ronald
N.
Bracewell at the
Radio
Astronomy
Institute at
Stanford.

Conklin reasoned that
if the earth is moving through an isotropic sea of radia-
tion,
the earth's velocity should cause the radiation to
appear stronger in the direction the earth is moving.

After making corrections for the known motions of the
earth,
any remaining anomaly would indicate the pre-
viously unknown motion of the earth and the entire
Galaxy.
Conklin made his measurements with two radio tele-
scopes
12,500 feet above sea level.

Reporting results in
the

British journal
Nature,
he said he found the postu-
lated difference in radiation strength in the direction of
the northern constellation
Canes
Venatici
[the hunting dogs].

The size of
the difference implies that the earth is moving in that
direction at
160,000 miles per hour.

L–14 = Luminiferous ether.

Or L–48 = 4 + 8 = 12:
L–12 = Luster.

An old-time eulogy wd say:
"The luster of your deeds
against the daddy-giant-bogeyman
will never fade or tarnish."

Alas!

An idle boast.

B–12 = Mercury lamplight.

At this point I write:
"To be continued . . ."

What do you think of
when you think of the light
of a mercury-vapor lamp?

Do you think of a pearly nothing light
or a bluish light
—or do you think of black light,
the lavender light
containing occult rays,
the rays beyond the violet light
that burn us unawares
& take our pictures?

The vapor of Mercury,
messenger of the gods,
excited the emanation
of invisible radiation.

"Just get back from Florida?"

"No.

New sunlamp."

$$\left\{ \begin{array}{l} \text{PURE COFFEE} \\ \text{O- 226 GRAMS—} \\ \text{DO NOT REFRIGERATE} \end{array} \right.$$

2+2 = 4+6 = 10:
O–10 = Amethyst light.
The day my wise old psychiatrist had his funeral,
with Tillich still alive & present

156

& Meyer Schapiro's personal eulogy,
interrupted by his tears,
but masterly setting forth
the accomplishments & wisdom of Kurt Goldstein,
that day,
after sadly shaking hands
with Charlotte & Hanon,
& beginning my return to work in midtown,
I passed the store on Madison in the 80's
where often I had bought
necklaces & earrings for Alexandra Hontchar
when I worked for
Unicorn in that neighborhood.

A small ring
with a purple stone—presumably an amethyst—
rested in the right-hand window
among the $3 specials.

Its tarnished silver mounting
was carved in grapy shapes;
I bought it then & wore it
in memory of my wise old friend.

A number of years later
I still wore it much of the time,
my "Goldstein's Funeral Ring."

(Even with a wedding ring?)

I'm not sure whether I still had it by the time
I was wearing a wedding ring.

(I didnt wear one myself
until several years after our marriage.

Now I no longer wear it:
it seems too little for my finger.)

But sometime a few years ago
2 Puerto Rican painter-plasterer-neighbors
were doing work in the kitchen at Hoe Avenue,
where the ring hung with a horseshoe-nail ring on a white hook.

It disappeared sometime around then.

The first amethyst I saw
Was in Hubbard's Woods
it must have been when I was 8 or less,
for we still lived on Chicago's South Side,
& my parents had made a rare family car trip
out to Hubbard's Woods
(the northern part of Winnetka,
just on the border of Glencoe)
to visit Ernie Peterman & his wife
—Ernie Peterman, my father's friend,
the chief refrigerating engineer at the North Shore Ice Co.,
just over the North Shore tracks in Glencoe,
of which Harry Roberts was the President:

Ernie Peterman,
whom my mother usually
referred to as "the Dutchman"
or "that Dutch iceman."

She used "Dutch" meaning "German,"
as in "Pennsylvania Dutch"
—I don't know whether this was Ohioan
or second-generation Jewish.

My mother's father,

blue-eyed blonde Jacob Baskin,
had come over from Odessa;
his red-haired
(was *she* blue-eyed too?)
wife,
from Austria-Hungary—
her name was Mary—
—was it, "Weiner,"
the same as Iris's mother's maiden name?
—I cannot trust my memory—
no, it was "Reicher"—
often spoke in her last years when we visited her
in Springfield or Columbus
of how she was being cheated
—"by the Jews."

The family ran a dry-goods store
in Springfield, Ohio,
from the time my mother was 12
(she'd been born in Cleveland
& the family had moved from town to town in Ohio
—I remember especially seeing the house they'd lived in
on Euclid Avenue, Yellow Springs—
setting up a kind of chain of stores, it seems,
until they got to Springfield
& her mother or my mother or all of them had said:
"This is it.
We aren't going to budge
from here on out."),
& she went to school
in that Lutheran town's
German-dominated public schools,
& later to college at Wittenberg
—like Hamlet—
but never having to leave German Springfield
(except for that summer or so
studying photoplaywriting at Columbia).

There German was taught

From the 3rd or 4th grade on in the public schools;
my mother taught it there
until she met my father in a hotel lobby,
had him home to meet the folks,
this dapper British travelling salesman,
(upward-middle-class Jewish
Cockney but still dapper
& able to crack a joke & tell a story then
or sing a song or recite a poem:
—"Gunga Din,"
or "The Wreck of the Raspberry Jam"
or one or more soliloquies of Hamlet),
& after I dont know how long a courting,
they crossed the Ohio River at Cincinnati
& were married,
for some reason I've never learned,
in Covington, Kentucky.

But this time instead of Daddy going out to Hubbard's Woods alone & getting drunk
with Ernie Peterman,
& maybe Harry Roberts,
we'd all come out to visit,
& Ernie Peterman
showed me a pin or ring with an amethyst in it.

I think it was a tiepin,
for when I reached for it,
thinking he was giving it to me,
someone explained
that that purple brightness
was much too expensive
to *give* away—
—or at least to give away right then to me;
but he did give me a tiepin
whose ivory head was carved a bloodless rose
half an inch or so across.

Now I have a chunk of amethyst

still adhering to the rock it grew on,
a gift several years ago
from poet-storyteller Spencer Holst,
my friend a quarter century this spring,
the last spring of the 1960's.

S–933-2220
9+3 = 12+3 = 15+2 = 17+2 = 19+2 = 21
S–21 = soft radiance

The soft radiance of Satyagraha
streams from the raucous deed of desanctification.

Truth force,
soul force,
love force,
the joyous confetti of personal truth
subsuming & transcending the stealing of documents,
subliming the stolen death paper,
melting the stolen "1" & "A" keys
of resting typewriters of death
—why didnt you also take
the key to ubiquitous "Ee"?—
lives in soft radiance
of unmalicious eyes
or ones whose humourous malice
is deadly-lovingly serious.

Softly radiant ladies
against gray Daddy Warbucks
(more gray than pinky-bald
in real life):
a Whistler composition in gold & gray
with fluttery white & green
& a vortex of viscous black

—a mess where a mess is needed:
right in the very center
of Rockefeller Center—
the lie given,
the oil spilt,
the dollars & death papers shredded,
the rebellious destructive deed openly avowed,

& now,* blessèd reprieve,   * 11 October 1969
the miraculous postponement of the consequences
by the black lady judge
who used to be Boro President of Manhattan!

Blessèd soft radiance
of serendipitous truth
(weeks or months of freedom yet
due to a technicality!)
mingles with the harder light
in which our social truth
lies summed in a mess of oil & dirty paper.

I see the soft friendly radiance of your eyes.

K–69 = 6+9 = 15
K–15 = comet light.

No, I'm not sure
whether or not I've seen a comet's light.

I think I did once,
pretty long ago,
but I'm not sure.

I cd talk like Stephen Spender
of your deed of gleeful destruction

162

"leaving the vivid air signed in your honor"
(I quote from memory, & as I said before,
my memory's not to be trusted).

No comets, you hoydens,
but sensibly angry women
doing their dirty best
(as biologically usual, alas)
to help preserve the ill-deserving species
Homo sapiens,
vertebrate worm of planets,
ruiner of all he sets his hands upon.

E–10/11/69 = 10+11 = 21+69 = 90 = 9

E–9 = electric lamplight.

I don't even know whether this "e" shd be here;
I don't even know
whether your name is "Boskey"
or "Bosky":

If it's "Boskey,"
the "e" leads me to reflect
that I'm writing this new light poem
early in the morning of Columbus Day,
1969,
at 965 Hoe Avenue in the Bronx,
in electric light,
in electric lamplight, even,
if, as many do,
you call electric bulbs "electric lamps."

I don't know whether the "e"
shd be here,

but I *do* know that your main mistake
was not taking those typewriters' "e" keys
as long as you were "taking a few things."

$$Y-1915 = 19+15 = 34 = 3+4 = 7$$
$$Y-7 = I -7 = \text{ice-sky light.}$$

The poem ends under an ice sky,
a sky with clouds
sparkling with tiny ice crystals,
brilliant sun behind them,
unavailing against the arctic winds
swimming across the skies,
covering with treacherous
whiteness
North
American vastness
as well as the mythical wastelands of Siberia.

The winter is coming.

The Weathermen, unneeded,
may be the fatal catalysts
that cause the supersaturated welter of America,
seemingly a-thawing now,
to freeze into a final shape of horror.

Jill, & you others,
desperate Resisters,
knights whose troubled violence
scorns to injure persons,
Oh you, my friends, of our peculiar "party,"
quibblers about means & ends,
worriers over purity of intention,
lovers of spontaneous improvisation,
talkers to policemen & soldiers,

who know today's "pig"
may be tomorrow's lion of Resistance
or Christlike tiger of transfiguring love
   (Lamb of God,
      who takes away the sins of the world,
      give us peace),
tightrope-walkers on the line of truth
who are the Lamb of God:

Take away the sins of the world!

Give us peace!

The ice sky sparkles us to hope.

29ᵗʰ Light Poem: *In Memoriam* Charles Olson—21 January–27 April 1970

First Movement of the Light:
The Refinding of Lost Time

In what kind of light
may I mourn
this man
I met, once, twenty-two years ago,
when he drove to New York from Washington,
borrowing Caresse Crosby's pink convertible,
to spend some time with Rexroth,
visiting here for a while from San Francisco?

I cd hardly believe that enormous man
had emerged from that delicate car!

I remember sitting in a restaurant,
like a chipmunk between two grizzly bears,
as they shouted & exploded at each other,
often seeming overbearing boors
to my melancholy, reticent, twenty-six-year-old self
of the fall of 1948,
but always radiating
magical energies,
transforming that drab public room
to a meeting place of jovial, scornful giants,
a jousting place of titans
armed with fiery words,
fiercely wrestling in their huge affection.

In what kind of light may I mourn
this poet,
whose works I admire but seldom read,
whose concerns often escape me,
even when closest to mine,
whose Gloucester I never really saw,

carried thru it at night in a police car
two months before I met him,
when, hitchhiking with Billy Fair to Rockport
from Boston,
to which we'd come, also by thumb, from Woodstock,
we'd been picked up by the Beverly cops,
who, after checking us out,
drove us to the town limits,
where the next town's police, summoned by radio,
carried us thru & did the same,
so we were passed along Cape Ann
from police car
to police car
by "The New England Free Taxi Service,"
as we called it when we'd got used to it
& to these suburban cops'
"objective friendliness,"
until the Gloucester cops
carried us thru & let us out in absolute darkness
on the deserted road to Rockport,
where, hours later in the early morning,
after we'd walked the rest of the night,
saintly Charlie Wellman,
who'd sometimes lived at my place on Avenue C,
gathering edible fruit & vegetables
from garbage outside groceries,
welcomed us to his mother's house,
apologetic for its "bourgeois" comfort:

for Charlie was "New Left" in the early 40's,
Harvard graduate,
rejected "the system" totally,
"opportunist," he called himself,
lived on what others threw out
to avoid & evade money,
symbol symptom of system evil,
—one-man-revolutionary
too far-out to be violent
or condemn fellow rebels for violence
—opportunistic

vegetarian
pacific anarchist:

a boyish man, in his thirties at least,
dutifully doing shopping for his mother,
tho he'd've shopped the trash piles in New York

(Charlie's mother's house
was old & clean & pleasant,
with tan-varnished woodwork dully shining)

—in what kind of light may I mourn the poet
whose death brought to life again
those days of late summer & fall
of 1948?

In the Light wherein Time that was lost is found again.

      *   *   *   *   *

Second Movement of the Light:
The Litany of the Beautiful Lights

May The Eternal Light shine on him.
May The One Light shine on him.
May The Light Accepting Repentance shine on him.
May The Last Light shine on him.
May The Abasing Light shine on him.
May The Prevailing Light shine for him.
May The Avenging Light shine for him.

May The Light Ruling The Kingdom shine about him.
May The Fashioning Light shine about him.
May The Majestic Light shine about him.
May The One Light shine about him.

May The Light shine above him.
May The Making Light shine above him.
May The Seeing Light shine above him.
May The Subtle Light shine above him.
May The Light shine above him.
May The Light That Withholds shine above him.

May The Subsisting Light shine under him.
May The Dominant Light shine under him.

*   *   *   *   *

May The Prevailing Light shine out from him.
May The Powerful Light shine out from him.
May The Pardoning Light shine out from him.
May The Hidden Light shine out from him.
May The Honoring Light shine out from him.

May The Deferring Light shine across him.
May The Kind Light shine across him.

May The Light Ruling The Kingdom shine upon him.
May The Forgiving Light shine upon him.
May The Generous Light shine upon him.
May The Eternal Light shine upon him.

May The Guiding Light shine past him.
May The Fashioning Light shine past him.
May The Ruling Light shine past him.

May The Light That Is Aware shine past him.
May The Guiding Light shine past him.
May The Distressing Light shine past him.

May The Finding Light shine after him.
May The Bestowing Light shine after him.

*   *   *   *   *

May The Light That Brings Forward shine in behalf of him.
May The Prevailing Light shine in behalf of him.
May The Kind Light shine in behalf of him.
May The Governing Light shine in behalf of him.
May The Destroying Light shine in behalf of him.

May The First Light shine below him.
May The Light Rules The Kingdom shine below him.

May The Light That Is Lord of Majesty And Liberality shine over him.
May The Dominant Light shine over him.
May The Watching Light shine over him.
May The Powerful Light shine over him.

May The Incomparable Light shine down on him.
May The Forgiving Light shine down on him.
May The Just Light shine down on him.
May The Clement Light shine down on him.
May The Incomparable Light shine down on him.

May The Glorious Light shine into him.
May The Providing Light shine into him.

*   *   *   *   *

NOTE: Each line of *The Litany of the Beautiful Lights* is to be read with normal statement intonation: at the end of the line, drop the voice to its lowest pitch & let it gradually fade away; then pause about half a second. At strophe breaks, the pause shd be extended to at least two seconds; at section breaks (asterisks), to at least five seconds.

While the *Litany* is to be read deliberately & calmly, with definite silences, an "immanent" emotion, engendered by the reader's intense concentration on the meaning of each line as he/she reads it, ought to become clearly audible.

The attributes of the Light in this litany were drawn from the ninety-nine "Beautiful Names" of (the attributes of) God, as Muḥammad calls them (Ḳur'ân, Surah vii, verse 179), as listed & translated on pp. 47–50 of *Amulets and Talismans*, by Sir. E.A.Wallis Budge (University Books, New Hyde Park, N.Y., 1961; the British edition, which seems to have been published about 1930, was entitled *Amulets and Superstitions*, tho Budge remarks in his preface that the last word ought more correctly to be "Magic").

The book itself came into my hands serendipitously while I was writing this poem: My duties as an instructor in the American Language Institute of NYU include interviewing foreign students after they take certain tests at beginnings of semesters. Since I'm seldom otherwise in the vicinity during the day, I took the opportunity between two interview sessions to go to Samuel Weiser's bookstore (near NYU on Broadway) to buy a certain kind of incense available there. As I was doing so, the poet Charles Stein came in, & we began a conversation, which was interrupted by a clerk, who asked me whether I'd like some books that he'd been asked to throw out because they were variously mutilated. When I said "Yes," he gave me several excellent volumes, some of which were only minimally mutilated, altho the copy of *Amulets and Talismans* has had pp. 365–442 (Chapters XXI–XXVI, on Ḳabballah, Astrology, & Numerology) cut out.

Further personal discoveries & decisions, as well as objective systematic-chance operations, led to the final form of the Litany. These I will not detail, but I wish thank to the poet Larry Fagan for having given an initial impetus to the setting down of the poem (which might otherwise remained an amorphous constellation of memories & feelings aroused by the death of Charles Olson) by inviting me to read at the memorial program for Mr. Olson at St. Marks in-the-Bouwerie Church (4 Feb. 1970). Since then, several revisions have been made in the first part of the poem, but the Litany has remained as read then, contrary to my original systematic-chance-determined program, which called for 13 more sections.

Performance instructions for 30th Light Poem: For Allan Kaprow (Road Signals)

Before the poem begins, the signals are placed in a circle or oval on tables or on the floor.

The poem is divided into 3 movements:

1.

During the 1st movement, use the *black or blue members* on the *larger* of your 2 sets of number cards to regulate your actions (numbers 1 to 20). Silently count the number on each card as "photographer's seconds" ("one thousand and one, one thousand and two, one thousand and three . . ."). Never hurry the counting. If anything, make each second longer than a clock second rather than shorter. At the end of the first time period, turn your signal on; at the end of the 2nd, turn it off, & so on. Discard each number card into a pocket as soon as it is used. During this 1st movement, move the signals occasionally from one place to another, *both* while they are on & while they are off.

2.

During the 2nd movement, use the *red numbers* on your *smaller* pack of number cards (numbers 21 to 120) to regulate your actions. Continue actions from 1st movement (since the signal is on at the end of the 1st, the 2nd movement begins with counting and then turning it off), Move the signal occasionally from one place to another, but *only when it is off.* At the end of the last period, turn the signal off & move it back to its original position.

3.

As soon as the signal is back in its original position, turn it on & leave it on continuously. One signal operator will count seconds or use a watch to measure a predetermined length of time. At the end of this period, the time-keeper turns his or her signal off. Each other operator then looks at the *red* (larger) number on one card, counts that number of seconds, & turns the signal off.

31st Light Poem: For the Central Regions of the Sun—30–31 May 1970

"The sun has to solve these equations in order
to qualify as a star.

If the sun has solved them,
so will we!"

temperature of
27
million degrees
Fahrenheit for the central regions of the sun.

the central regions of the sun.

27
million degrees
Fahrenheit for the central regions of the sun.

sun.

sun.

central regions of the sun.

HENRY JAMES HAD
had his first attack of gout.

Fahrenheit for the central regions of the sun.

his first attack of gout.

temperature of
27
million degrees
Fahrenheit for the central regions of the sun.

for the central regions of the sun.

sun.

for the central regions of the sun.

million degrees
Fahrenheit for the central regions of the sun.

convert a pint of water into energy
we could supply all the power needed on the
Earth each day for light-
ing,
heating,
and heavy industry.

temperature of
27
million degrees
Fahrenheit for the central regions of the sun.

temperature of
27
million degrees
Fahrenheit for the central regions of the sun.

the central regions of the sun.

27
million degrees
Fahrenheit for the central regions of the sun.

first attack of gout.

temperature of
27
million degrees
Fahrenheit for the central regions of the sun.

energy
we could supply all the power needed on the
Earth each day for light-
ing
heating,
and heavy industry.

equally acceptable?

gout.

attack of gout.

27
million degrees
Fahrenheit for the central regions of the sun.

light-
ing,
heating,
and heavy industry.

astronomer turns from the sun to the stars his problem is
a little more difficult.

religion."

particles suspended in the chromo-
sphere of the star,
and by analyzing the dark absorption lines we can
identify the various elements,
making a rather exact chemical analy-
sis.

into energy
we could supply all the power needed on the
Earth each day for light-
ing,
heating,
and heavy industry.

into energy
we could supply all the power needed on the
Earth each day for light-
ing,
heating,
and heavy industry.

of
27

million degrees
Fahrenheit for the central regions of the sun.

from the sun to the stars his problem is
a little more difficult.

HAD
had his first attack of gout.

JAMES HAD
had his first attack of gout.

central regions of the sun.

temperature of
27
million degrees
Fahrenheit for the central regions of the sun.

for the central regions of the sun.

queens.

heating,
and heavy industry.

million degrees
Fahrenheit for the central regions of the sun.

million degrees
Fahrenheit for the central regions of the sun.

significance of the series.

equally acceptable?

a pint of water into energy
we could supply all the power needed on the
Earth each day for light-
ing,
heating,

and heavy industry.

astronomer turns from the sun to the stars his problem is
a little more difficult.

a pint of water into energy
we could supply all the power needed on the
Earth each day for light-
ing,
heating,
and heavy industry.

sun.

attack of gout.

heating,
and heavy industry.

degrees
Fahrenheit for the central regions of the sun.

into energy,
we could supply all the power needed on the
Earth each day for light-
ing,
heating,
and heavy industry.

of
27
million degrees
Fahrenheit for the central regions of the sun.

temperature of
27
million degrees
Fahrenheit for the central regions of the sun.

the central regions of the sun.

27
million degrees
Fahrenheit for the central regions of the sun.

sun.

sun.

sun.

central regions of the sun.

HENRY JAMES HAD
had his first attack of gout.

Fahrenheit for the central regions of the sun.

his first attack of gout.

sun.

for the central regions of the sun.

million degrees
Fahrenheit for the central regions of the sun.

convert a pint of water into energy
we could supply all the power needed on the
Earth each day for light-
ing,
heating,
and heavy industry.

temperature of
27
million degrees
Fahrenheit for the central regions of the sun.

needed on the
Earth each day for light-
ing,

heating,
and heavy industry.

temperature of
27
million degrees
Fahrenheit for the central regions of the sun.

the central regions of the sun.

27
million degrees
Fahrenheit for the central regions of the sun.

from the sun to the stars his problem is
a little more difficult.

sun.

for the central regions of the sun.

water into energy
we could supply all the power needed on the
Earth each day for light-
ing,
heating,
and heavy industry.

million degrees
Fahrenheit for the central regions of the sun.

million degrees
Fahrenheit for the central regions of the sun.

million degrees
Fahrenheit for the central regions of the sun.

water into energy
we could supply all the power needed on the
Earth each day for light-
ing,

heating,
and heavy industry.

temperature of
27
million degrees
Fahrenheit for the central regions of the sun.

Note: From p. 164 (lower middle-2nd paragraph ending is the title) to p. 166 (near bottom),
Gerald S. Hawkins: *Splendor in the Sky* (Harper & Row, revised ed.: 1969) & pp. 19–28, Leon Edel, *Henry James*. Vol. 4: *The Treacherous Years: 1895–1901*, Lippincott, Philadelphia & New York, 1969

32nd Light Poem: For the O & the B Stars, the Blue & the Pale-Blue ones
    —3 November 1970

    Assembled by Jackson Mac Low from pp. 166 ff., *Splendor in the Sky*, by Gerald S. Hawkins
    (Lippincott, Phila. & NY, rev. ed., 1969)

On a clear moonless night you can see more than two thousand
stars,
and with a telescope the number jumps into the millions.

The
work of the astronomer would never end if all these stars were differ-
ent.

If stars showed as many individual traits and variations as people,
for example,
a complete survey would be impossible.

Fortunately the
millions of stars can be arranged in eight broad classes,
according to
their spectral type or color.

We use the letters of the alphabet to dis-
tinguish between one star and the next,
but there was much argument,
discussion,
and changing of minds before the system was finally
established.

The letters have therefore finished up in some disorder:
        O B A F G K M N

[This poem is incomplete and was abandoned in favor of a 32nd Light Poem for Paul Blackburn. —Eds.]

32nd Light Poem: *In Memoriam* Paul Blackburn—9–10 October 1971

Let me choose the kinds of light
to light the passing of my friend
Paul Blackburn   a poet

A pale light like that of a winter dawn
or twilight
or phosphorescence

is not enough to guide him in his passing
but enough for us to see
shadowily his last gaunt figure

how he showed himself to us
last July in Michigan
when he made us think he was recovering

knowing the carcinoma
arrested in his esophagus
had already spread to his bones

How he led us on
I spent so little time with him
thinking he'd be with us now

Amber light of regret
stains my memories of our days
at the poetry festival in Allendale Michigan

How many times I hurried elsewhere
rather than spending time with him
in his room 3 doors from me

I will regret it the rest of my life
I must learn to live
with the regret

dwelling on the moments
Paul & I shared
in July as in years before

tho amber light dim to umber
& I can hardly see
his brave emaciated face

I see Paul standing in the umber light
cast on his existence
by his knowing that his death was fast approaching

Lightning blasts the guilty dream
& I see him
reading in the little auditorium

& hear him
confidently reading
careful of his timing

anxious not to take
more than his share of reading time
filling our hearts with rejoicing

seeing him alive
doing the work he was here for
seemingly among us now

I for one was fooled
thinking he was winning the battle
so I wept that night for joy

As I embraced him after he read
I shook with relief & love
I was so happy to hear you read again

If there were a kind of black light
that suddenly cd reveal to us
each other's inwardness

what wd I have seen that night
as I embraced you
with tears of joy

I keep remembering the bolt of lightning
that slashed the sky at twilight
over the Gulf of St. Lawrence

& turned an enchanted walk with Bici
following Angus Willie's Brook
thru mossy woods nearly to its mouth

to a boot-filling scramble up thru thorn bush & spruce tangle
Beatrice guided me & I was safe
at the end of August on Cape Breton Island

but when Jerry telephoned me of your death
the lightning that destroyed
the illusion you were safe

led thru dreadful amber light
not to friendly car light
& welcoming kitchen light

but the black light of absence
not ultraviolet light
revealing hidden colors

but revelatory light that is *no* light
the unending light of the realization
that no light will ever light your bodily presence again

Now your poems' light is all
The unending light of your presence
in the living light of your voice

33rd Light Poem: *In Memoriam* Leonard Hicks—6–9 November 1971

Don't turn up the footlights
Don't turn on the following spot
The Superior Man
is not here

We are here
trying to say something
unpolluted
by sentimentality

It's hard to speak of the dead
It's hard to speak of death
Death is a mystery
Death is a mystery

Death is a mystery
is a banal thing to say
As banal as
Death is a tragedy

Death is not always a tragedy
but it is always
a mystery
Death is a mystery

I put this banal truth
in the limelight
because it has been borne in on me
by the recent deaths of friends

by the death of Leonard Hicks
by the death of Paul Blackburn
by the death of Jennie Hecht
by the death of the Rev. Bill Maloney

Leonard and Paul by cancer
Jennie by an overdose of heroin
Bill by an artery's bursting
What is the mystery

The foreign pre-med students
who study English with me
insist there is no mystery
you die and rot away

They can see no mystery in death
The soul stops being because the brain stops
They wouldn't say Soul but Mind
The Mind's a function of the brain and dies with it

I put mystery in the limelight
and use the banal phrase
Put in the limelight
because I've gotten out my chart of lights

Some say Limelight now for any spotlight
though few use the word at all now
except in the cliché
and no one uses a real limelight

No one uses a lens
to concentrate the light produced
by directing an oxyhydrogen flame
upon a cylinder of lime

but Limelight came into the poem
because Leonard begins with an L
and Leonard was an actor
and Limelight appears in the L-column of the chart

Does this trivialize your requiem
you tall broad-shouldered man with the gaunt face
who worked so hard
all the time I knew you

I never knew what you thought of the way I wrote
My need to elaborate strategies of chance
to do my writing for me
Yet I knew you over more than a decade

And you were drafted by the Becks
to act in *The Marrying Maiden*
the role of the Superior Man
each of whose lines had only two words or phrases in it

You probably thought
and probably rightly
it all was an ego trip
disguised as selflessness

But in theater ego-tripping has to be forgiven
It's so naively blatant and the rule there
And mine   I hope   wasn't destructive
So I think you forgave it

as you forgave directorial indignities
Your head was upside down when I first saw you
Delivering lines with your head hanging over the head of a bed
in Picasso's silly surrealist farce *Desire*

The Living Theatre at the Cherry Lane in '53
They called it An Evening of Bohemian Theatre
Stein's *Ladies' Voices* and Eliot's *Sweeney Agonistes*
formed a trio with the Picasso

It was a popular bill they kept reviving
My first Living Theatre role
was that summer in its last revival
Krumpacker in *Sweeney*   without a rehearsal

Now when I remember your head
saying those lines upside down
I see the inverted head in Guernica
below the light lamp held by a bodiless arm

I want to light some lights for you Leonard
I want to be able to say how kind you were
I want to say what a good workman you were
acting or fixing plumbing or making plates at the *Daily News*

Fornés said it all in the *Voice* last week
I'll always love her for writing so much of the truth about you
She's left me little to do
but light one flickering candle for your mighty flame.

34ᵗʰ Light Poem: *In Memoriam* Jennie Hecht—27–28 November 1971

Jennie in Jade light
telling the Tarot
she died of an overdose of downers

Jennie so full of life
she seemed too small to contain it all
she died of an overdose of downers

Jennie I'm cutting the cards
with the bare electric lightbulb
burning overhead

Jennie I've cut to the Empress
The passive power of the material world
A force against which one cannot react

Jennie you could no longer react
against the passive power of matter
You died of an overdose of downers

Jennie I'm cutting the cards
I'm only using the Major Arcana
The Judgment comes down like a Meteorite

Jennie you were called to the higher state
You wanted to raise yourself to a higher plane
You died of an overdose of downers

Jennie you raised our hearts to a higher state
your eager being made us all more alive
Thinking of you dead is like thinking a black sun

Jennie I've cut to the Fool
He doesn't have a number
He's neither high nor low

Jennie the Fool can be progressing toward evolution
or thoughtlessness   lack of order
carelessness in promises   insecurity

Jennie you danced at the brink of the abyss
The natural light streamed down all around you
Nobody expected your foot to slip

Jennie I shuffle & cut to Justice
sitting with sword & scales on a throne
This is the image of equilibrium

Jennie a pile of wood was on one pan
An igniter lit it and its counterweight crashed down
as the wood burned to ashes and the ashes blew away

Jennie it's the Pope That's a laugh
What is the Pope doing in your poem
He is occult power & a secret revealed

Jennie you revealed the secrets of the Tarot
You were the only one who made the Tarot speak to me
The Pope's on the moon grinning in earthlight

Jennie the Empress is here again
The force of matter we can't beat
Simone Weil's Downdrag heavy heavy heavy

Jennie it's a heavy negative light
The light that drags all livingness to death
The Empress is downer light

Jennie it's the World now
The perfection of man but the negation of feelings
As if perfection took place in an eclipse

Jennie the birds fly away
but there's the statue standing
as the eerie winds of midday darkness rise

Jennie the Magician's here
He performs in candlelight
We can't tell whether he's for real or not

Jennie you loved to perform in candlelight
doing real magic with the cards
struggling with the undercurrents of the occult

Jennie you juggled in the currents
till chance brought about
the last change of all

Jennie all I can remember is you speaking
with the words tumbling out of your mouth upside down
& your eyes flashing light I cannot imagine lost

Jennie the Tower of Destruction has appeared
The unexpected shock of your death
The tower struck by lightning

Jennie the Hermit says there's a secret to be revealed
Does the mystery of death hold such a secret
The absence of the light of your face mocks the questioner

35th Light Poem: For Charlie Morrow—A Tape Piece for Him to Realize—6 December 1971

Repeat each line of a poem for a certain duration interspersed w/ silences of certain durations.

The series of line repetitions begin sequentially (in the order given in the text) but each new series begins & proceeds simultaneously with all the other series that began before it; i.e., line 1 begins and repeats, and while it is repeating, line 2 begins and is repeated along with the repetitions of line 1; then line 3 begins & repeats while lines 1 & 2 continue to repeat, & so on.

A B C D E F G H I J K L M N O P Q R S T U V W X Y Z
A B♭ C D E F G B♮ C♯ D♯ E♯ F♯ G♯ A♯ B♯ C♭ D♭ E♭ F♭ G♭ A♭ B♭ G F D C♭

Each *entrance* of a line of words & a tone is forte.

Each line is recorded along with a continuous tone in natural (not tempered) intonation. (A=440) The name of the "tone class" is given (e.g., "C♮") but the person realizing the tape is free to choose the register of the tone (e.g., "middle C," "high C," etc.).

Make each line into a loop in which there is a slight pause in the *speech* after the last word, but in which the *tone* accompanying the words is continuous. Start the tone generator *before* the words begin and let it run a short time after the words

e.g.,

Tone (C♮) | ——————————————————————————— |

Words |–^(S)–| A "C" : A "C natural" in candlelight. |–^(S)–|

1 second of the tone before and after words.

2 track Stereo: each line & tone enters (*f*) on an alternate track: i.e., line one enters on track 1; line two on track 2; line 3 on track 1; line 4 on track 2; etc. However, after each duration of silence, the line & tone reenter (if it does) on the other track, i.e., line one reenters on track 2; line 2 reenters on track 1; etc. After their second durations of silence, each line & tone reenters (if it does) on the original track. Line 13 enters on both tracks & continues on both till the end.

One way is to record each line of words alone with a second of silence before & after the words. Then, with each re-entrance of the loop, feed a tone of the required class, but in a different register—e.g., the 1st minute might have a middle "C" accompanying the spoken words, then after 2 minutes of silence, the 3rd, 4th, & 5th minutes might have a high "C"; and the final 5 minutes might have a very low "C"— a tone is fed onto the track directly from the sound generator.

The words and sound score for "35ᵗʰ Light Poem: For Charlie Morrow"

1	C♮	A "C" : a "C natural" in candlelight
		1'R – 2'S – 3'R – 4'S – 5'R
2	B♮	An "H" : a "B natural" in hot light
		2'S – 3'R – 4'S – 5'R – 1'S
3	A♮	An "A" : an "A natural" in the light of an arc-light
		3'S – 4'R – 5'S - 1'R – 2'S
4	E♭	An "R" : an "E flat" in radiance
		4'S – 5'R – 1'S – 2'R – 3'S
5	F♯	An "L" : an "F sharp" in light
		5'S – 1'R – 2'S – 3'R – 4'S
6	C♯	An "I" : a "C sharp" in light of incandescence
		6'S – 4'R – 3'S – 2'R
7	E♮	An "E" : an "E natural" in eclipse light
		7'S – 1'R – 2'S – 3'R – 2'S
8	G♯	An "M" : a "G sharp" in the light of a match flame
		8'S – 2'R – 3'S – 2'R
9	B♯	An "O" : a "B sharp" in the light of an oil lamp
		9'S – 1'R – 2'S – 3'R
10	E♭	An "R" : an "E flat" in reflected light
		10'S – 4'R – 1'S
11	E♭	An "R" : an "E flat" in the light of a rainbow
		11'S – 2'R – 1'S – 1'R
12	B♯	An "O" : a "B sharp" in owl light
		12'S – 1'R – 1'S – 1'R
13	G♮	A "W" : a "G natural" in waxing light.
		13'S – 2'R

[The letters and numerals in the chart are defined as follows:

  1'S represents one minute of silence
  1'R represents one minute of repetitions

  2'S represents two minutes of silence
  2'R represents two minutes of repetitions, and so on.
                                        —Eds.]

36th Light Poem: *In Memoriam* Buster Keaton—4:50–6:18 AM 1 January 1972

1

As a Mad Scientist
Buster lights a Bunsen-burner flame
that starts a series of processes
that eventually releases The Monster

As an Undertaker
Buster lights a Bunsen-burner flame
that starts a series of processes
that awakens a drunk who was about to be buried as a corpse

As a Muscovite
Buster lights a sisal wick in a sesame-seed-oil lamp
that suddenly lights a mystical orgy
officiated over by Rasputin

As a Boater
Buster beats a cascade by floating out beyond its edge
borne by a balloon
lit by a wintry sun

As an Unwilling Passenger on a Drifting Liner
Buster the Millionaire & his rich Girl Friend
learn to cope Alone Without Servants
when forced to rely on the light of their Upper-Class Intellects

As a Worker
Buster arouses the Compassion of the Nation
in whose light the Corporations
sell themselves to their Workers

As a Key Man
Buster carried around with him
an enormous bunch of keys
lighting his way with a Keats lamp

As a Beatnik
Buster meditates in a Redwood forest
seated where the Selenic light
first falls at Moonrise

As a Leaf-&-Feather Gatherer
Buster Means Well but bugs everyone in the Park
spearing the ladies' hats & the picknickers' salads
in featureless Hollywood Light of the century's first quarter

As William Butler Yeats
Buster addresses an irate Irish crowd
that thinks that Poetry makes Nothing Happen
but lets itself be bathed by its Truthful Light

As a Cannoneer
Buster explodes his own ship's magazine
treads water in Gunpowder Light at a safe distance
& blushes in embarrassment at his Clumsiness

As a Violinist
Buster surpasses Paganini
until Boston-Concert-Hall Light
Poisons him with Love for a Proper Bostonian Maiden

2

Spirit of Buster Keaton
if you survive as yourself
receive Please our honor & praise
you conscientious Workman

Hard-working Buster Keaton
when you arouse the laughter of children
as you live in Projector Light
Your Karmic Residue dissolves in Joyous Shouts

37th Light Poem: For Marguerite & Moses Harris—10 February–14 March 1972

Have you ever seen the midnight sun
Marguerite?

I've never seen the midnight sun
but I can imagine it
from the night of the northern lights
the summer of '71 on Cape Breton Island
when Bici & I came out of our tent
naked after lovemaking under one blanket
(at least that's how I remember it)
and watched the lights
proscenium'd first between clouds and horizon
over the Gulf of St Lawrence
then filling the sky
more & more
as the clouds were blown away over our heads
like the roof of a theatre being rolled back
revealing the sky
all of it over the Gulf
filled with Aurora Borealis.

And also from city skies
Filled with artificial light
"enough to read a newspaper by."

Moses and Marguerite
have you ever seen the light
of a roof lamp?

I used to have a roof lamp
when I lived on Avenue C in the middle '50s
I used to use the roof
as an outdoor living room in the summer
(imagine doing that now
on Avenue C between 9th & 10th!)
& brought an electric line up
from the top floor hall light socket
& had some lamp up there
either a standing lamp—a "bridge lamp"

or a goosenecked student lamp
& used to get high on pot & read or question the *I Ching*
using kitchen matches for yarrow stalks
or very short   three-or-four-inch lengths of yarrow stalk
or write poetry
until I'd fall asleep
under the stars & the soot
from the 14th-Street-&-the-river Con Edison plant

After I turned the light of my roof lamp out
I'd lie & watch the stars
until I fell asleep

just as I used to watch the stars
through the triangular tent window
that summer on Cape Breton
as I lay beside Bici
sleeping after making love with me

I used to lie & watch the stars as I fell asleep
buoyant with sexual happiness
under sheet blankets & spread out sleeping bag
beside her in the chilly tent
the same tent from which Geoff hailed us
to come out & see the lights
after we'd fallen asleep or maybe before
for our candle was still on
& our tent glowed like an orange lantern
I learned from Michael the other day
as we talked about that night of the Northern lights
the night before Bici & he
had to fly back to New York
the last night she shared that tent with me

Moses & Marguerite
Marguerite & Moses
I felt so loving toward you both
earlier tonight
when I stopped by to get the children's clothes
your friend had left with you for us
you both seemed to glow

bathed with or giving off—I couldn't tell which
a very good light
a light that made me glad we are friends

but as I write this poem for you
guided both by chance
& the once-avoided light of the unconscious
I find I fall into reminiscence
triggered by the light names
drawn from the old chart
by the letters of your names
& the numbers
three seven and ten
so far

O the evanescent light of reminiscence!
It comes & it goes
bathing first one time & place & then another
the headlight of our only time machine

I'm travelling in time tonight (it's after midnight now)
sitting alone in my kitchen
with the oven on for heat
smoking pot alone
at my square low kitchen table
covered by red oil cloth
on top of it the two-volume Wilhelm-Baynes *I Ching*
on it, a memo pad
on which I noted   was it *last* night?
Fêng Abundance Fullness
with a 9 in the third place
which makes it change to CHÊN
The Arousing Shock Thunder
which seems to mean what Reich meant by "Orgone"

No it was 2:15 Tuesday morning
now it's near one
Friday morning
11 February 1972

The memo pad before I pulled it out just now

to see what I'd written on it
(the date & time at the top
the two hexagrams
FÊNG & CHÊN
Chên over Li turning to Chên over Chên
as the unbroken line in the third place
changes to a broken line
a "nine" in the third place
the constituent trigrams' names
the hexagram's numbers in the series of 64
"55" & "51"
"9 in 3rd"
& "FÊNG
ABUNDANCE
FULLNESS"
under "Chên" over "Li"
"55" and "9 in 3rd"
under the left hexagram:

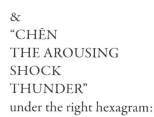

&
"CHÊN
THE AROUSING
SHOCK
THUNDER"
under the right hexagram:

I didn't ask a question
just asked
with the set of 10-inch-long yarrow stalks
Sam Reifler sent me nearly two years ago
bound with two thin strips of brown suede
each strip held together around the yarrow
one near each end of the stalks
by half a square knot

Now they're on the books on the window
propped on that wonderful book
Djuna Barnes' *Ryder*
the bottom of the bundle of stalks
(covered with a blue bandanna
wrapped scroll like about them

with its ends lapped over
& held with doubled wide rubber bands
at about the same places as
the suede strips inside)
the upper end propped in the corner
between the tile wall
& the molding at the far left of the window frame

I was going to tell you all the other things on my table
the radio the cereal the vitamin pills
the banana & peanuts in a bowl
the kleenex & the children's drawing paper
the light brown sugar box
& the jug of rosé leftover from
Clarinda's birthday party
the pot & the coffee cup
the wine glass & the pipes
one of wood 3 inches by 1 1/8 by 1/2
I made myself years ago
from a leftover piece of wood
It's black & brown & tan
with blackened tinfoil inset in the center
around the small bowl
& a hole at each end
so the air can cool the smoke
& a 3/8-inch square cut out of the right corner
of the end farther from the bowl
cut out of a red-brown knot
to make a 3/4-inch mouthpiece
the other a water pipe
consisting of a red plastic box
3 1/8 inches by 1 1/8 by 1 1/8
with a rubber stopper
in a hole in the top of the lid
& a blue-wooden-tipped brass mouthpiece
emerging at a 45° angle from one stopper hole
and a brass bowl & its stem rising from the other hole

There's a white spool of shiny pink thread on the table
Mordecai sewed a cuff button
on his red (mostly) plaid

cotton flannel shirt with it
all by himself yesterday morning

Tonight he mended an underarm seam rip
in the blue coverall with the "Fire Dept" patch on its sleeve
you gave me from your friend
along with all those clothes Clarinda loves
(or just likes the coverall the sneakers
& the red "baseball" zipper jacket)

I won't tell you all the things
on my table

I've spelled your name out Marguerite
up to the 2nd "r"
which I guess brings back
the light of a roof lamp

I was scared even then
when I slept all night on the roof
in May and June of 1955

But despite the soot
& the muted fear of intruders
I loved to watch the stars over the river
as I fell asleep on the roof
of 152 Avenue C
after I turned off the roof lamp
that late spring & early summer of 1955

It's 2:36 AM

2

That was 2:36 AM
the 11th of February 1972
Now glaring incandescent-lamp light
streams upon me from the shadeless table lamp
with a base like a brass tea kettle
or an overturned brass bowl
whose bare bulb is backed

by a sheet of aluminum foil
held against the molding
at the left side of the right kitchen window

the lamp's hung from the woodwork
between the two windows
in such a way that its bulb
is in front of the upper left corner
of the lower half of the right one
with foil between bulb and pane

WQXR-FM
just went off the air

It's after 2 AM
Tuesday the 14th of March 1972

38th Light Poem: For Daria—19 February 1972

A dazzling light?

Oh Daria
not in the usual sense of the word
not dazzling to the eyes
Dazzling to the heart
in the usual sense of the word

That's the light I see you in
A quiet aureole
that leaves the eyes alone as it passes through them to the heart
Making it shudder with tenderness

That's the light I see you in
remembering you
sitting in our living room last year
after Mordecai's birthday party
speaking and making music

Is the light of reminiscence
a kind of refracted light?

And if it is
What is the refracting medium?

& what is the source of illumination?

How can I see second scenes
along with what my eyes see?

You in our living room
& at the school the night of the play
& at the farm in Connecticut
in the spring

Your images supervening
on my cluttered kitchen table
with its red oilcloth cover
top left a pad of paper with a child's calligraphy

letters & arabic figures
& designs derived from them
on top a granola booklet
left center a blue & white tissue box
with a name & phone number propped against it
Nearer a mottled blue sugar bowl
with its mottled coral & gold-edged mouth
which I saw just now for the first time
to be a wide-open mouth
in which sits a silver cover with a black plastic knob
The cover's the shape of the scalp of a four or five inch sphere
one of the arctic regions
The knob's a small inverted truncated cone
its upturned base surmounted
by shallow concentric circular steps
If you count the cone base as one
There're three to the central platform
a quarter-inch circle whose surface is slightly curved
reflecting the curve of the metal it rises from

When I saw the open coral-lipped mouth
of the little blue sugar bowl
that has raw sugar in now
I noticed how tarnished the metal cover was
and burnished it at the sink
even unscrewing the knob
to polish the center better
& put the demitasse spoon
I use for a sugar spoon
into the bowl with its handle protruding
thru the tiny Romanesque near Moorish circle
cut in the edge of the metal

The bowl's got four slight indentations
running down its tapering blue sides
Maybe it's supposed to be a flower
Maybe a blue tulip
On each side there's a slanting line
incised in the blue & following down
the curve of the edge of one of the lips
A blue tulip-shape

with a base coming out
More than a quarter of an inch
tapered toward the table
a circle with four dents
below the subtle dents in the bowl's blue body
A kind of shallow clover shape
below the bowl's belly

A blue tulip
with wide open coral gold-edged lips

Oh yes
Why bother to mention the other things on the table?

The light of your remembered aureole
bathes my little glazed ceramic bowl
inside of whose silver cover
I see MADE IN ENGLAND
E.P.N.S.
whatever that means

I take the demitasse spoon out
rinse it off
& put it in the drainer rack
pour the raw sugar
into one of my new plain water glasses
& wash the bowl

Those small reddish spots on the bottom
of the cream-colored inside
are in the glaze

On the blue outer bottom of the bowl
stamped in green
not quite in the center
is a circle:
ROYAL WINTON
A —
inside of it
GRIM VADES (that's what it looks like
MADE IN
ENGLAND

I dry the bowl with yellow kitchen paper
& refill it from the glass
of tan turbinado sugar
Seven eighths of a glass of sugar
fills three quarters of the bowl
or thereabouts

I get the demitasse spoon
dry now
from the drainer
stick it down in the sugar
till tip touches bottom
& put the shiny cover on
arch over handle

A thin tapering tongue
broadest at its rounded tip
narrowing toward its root
protrudes thru the arch
across the coral lining of a lip
across a coral-lined lip
across a coral lip

"Le Rossignol en Amour" of Couperin
played on a silver flute
is on the radio
when I turn it on
after I finish a light poem
for Daria
whose other name I can't remember
whose remembered image stirs me deeply

39th Light Poem: For Kathy Acker

Kathy Acker
the better I know you
the more I admire you
Talking to you in a light poem
is like seeing you
in Kinetoscopic light

[Unfinished, undated, uncorrected, and erased with purple crayon. —Eds.]

40th Light Poem: for George Quasha—4 June 1972

Just now I was sure
I heard Iris call my name
I thought she was back with our kids
after she & they & Bici & her kids
& Bici's roomer Nicole
& her kid
had stayed until closing time
or thereabouts
in the Botanical Gardens
they went to see the Iris garden
hundreds ? of varieties of Iris
blooming now
around the back I think it is
of the main conservatory

Just now I thought I heard her call my name
& guiltily I put away the pot pipes
Why was I ashamed to be smoking pot all alone here?
Why did I turn on
the ventilator fan over the stove
Guilt is my middle ? no my first name

& your name's George

No G's on the light chart
I know without looking
I'll open a book on the human aura
lent to me by Clayton Eshleman
The Human Aura
by Walter J. Kilner
B.A., M.B. (Cantab.), M.R.C.P., etc.
Late Electrician to St. Thomas's Hospital, London

Hardly any G's in the index
Gallstones, and the aura, 261–62
Gamboge, 146
Gestation: early signs of, in the
        aura, 291–94; influence of, on the
        aura, after 4th or 5th month,
        297–98

What's Gamboge?

Yep it's a color

1. Gamboge,
complementary colour,
Prussian Blue.

2. Antwerp Blue,
complementary colour,
Gamboge.

3. Carmine,
complementary colour,
Emerald Green.

4. Emerald Green,
complementary colour,
Carmine.

> Each observer should if possible select
> by experi-
> ment what colour or colours suit him best.

In routine work,
use can be made of strips of
coloured paper three inches long and three quarters
of an inch in width with a black dot in the centre,
pasted on black board.

Experience has shown that
this is the largest size that can be conveniently
employed,
since a longer object does not yield the
complementary colour perfect to the ends.

With a
patient standing a few feet in front of the observer,
one of these strips will give a band of the complemen-
tary colour which,
when used transversely,

A soldier for international freedom
speaks from a Newark FM station
of life & revolution in Mozambique
& now Newark's mayor Kenneth Gibson
speaks with a panel about education
& Mrs Del Toro speaks Puerto Rican English
telling about the program
for Spanish-speaking children
the situation of the Spanish child
throughout the United States
has been a tragic one
instruction's given in Spanish in Newark
with English as a second language
& at the end of five years
the child will be bi-lingual
in culture
& language
Increased self image

will be
wider than the body,
allowing the ends that are
projected on each side beyond the body to be com-
pared with one another,
and also with the central
portion of the body itself.

       In winter or foggy weather,

There's a thunderstorm
a hard-blowing rain-slapping-down
thunder-&-lightning storm
going on outside

especially in London,

the difficulty of using paper strips for obtaining the
subjective complementary colours is great,
and it is
occasionally impossible to make a thorough examina-
tion from the inordinate time required,
which is
exceedingly trying to both the investigator and the
patient.

To overcome this defect an apparatus has
been devised,
which can be used in daylight or,
in an
emergency,
even by gaslight.

It consists of a cylin-
drical mask about six inches long and five in width,
with one end shaped to fit the face,
while the other has
a revolving cap in which there is an oblong slit three
quarters of an inch in breadth.

The slit can thus be
turned either horizontally or vertically to the eyes at
pleasure.

Behind the slit is placed a piece of ground
glass,
and at the back of this again a transparent
screen,
which may be either a cell containing a fluid
or else a piece of stained glass.

The mask ought to be
blackened inside or else lined with velvet.

A small
mark can be made on the ground glass to act in a
similar way as the dot on the coloured papers.

The
distance between the eyes and the screen will be about
correct for emmetropic sight,
but for presbyopia and
myopia the reading glasses worn by the observer will
be needed.

The writer's personal apparatus has a
removable diaphragm with lenses of the same focal
length as the spectacles he usually employs.

The distance between the eyes and the screen
is rather less than the ordinary
reading distance,
producing a slight strain of the eyes
which has been found
beneficial in practice.

      To use the apparatus,
it is only necessary to hold
it in front of and close to the face,
and to gaze at the
light,
keeping the eyes fixed on the mark on the
ground glass.

In a few seconds the eyes will have
become sufficiently affected,
and the complementary
coloured band can be perceived
in the same manner
as if the coloured papers had been used.

The appar-
atus requires more skill in using
than the coloured
papers,
as the screen needs alteration in depth of
colour according to the brightness of the light.

      As soon as the patient is ready for examination,
he should stand in front of a white background

opposite the light and illuminated evenly all over.
Should there be any shadows on the background they
must be made to correspond on the two sides.

Pre-
ferably the light should be brighter than when the
aura itself is being inspected,
but almost always it
will be necessary for one blind to be partially or
wholly drawn down.

After everything has been
properly arranged,
the observer must look at the sky
through the transparent screen in the mask,
or stare
at one of the coloured paper strips,
keeping his eyes
fixed on the dot from twenty to thirty
seconds accord-
ing to the brightness of the light.

          When coloured strips are used a brilliant
light is
required,
so it will be necessary to pull aside the blind
to allow the paper to be fully illuminated.

The
observer then turns toward the patient
and looks at
some predetermined spot on the median line of the
body,
when,
if used transversely,
the complementary
coloured band will be seen reaching
across the body
and extending to the background on either side,
the
whole being simultaneously visible.

He is thus
enabled to notice variations in the shades of the
colour in every part of the band.

The tints of the
extensions of the band prolonged beyond
the trunk
can be compared with each other,
but of course not
with the portion on the body itself.

The above-
mentioned method,
although simple,
requires a con-
siderable amount of practice,
and the mastery of one
or two details,
trifling in themselves,
will assist greatly
in speed and comfort.

First,
while looking at the
coloured strip,
it is indispensable to fix the eyes on one
particular spot and keep this in exact
focus the whole
time,
as unless this is properly done
there will be
blurring and an increase of time needed
for obtaining
the requisite effect.

A slight exercise of will is re-
quired for this,
but practice will soon make the effort
almost involuntary.

Secondly,

a novice often ex-
periences a difficulty
in keeping his eyes on a given
place on the patient's body,
owing to the proneness of
the complementary coloured band to wander,
often
out of the field of vision,
and for the eyes to follow it,
thus completely destroying the value of the obser-
vation.

When the habit of keeping the eyes station-
ary on one point has been acquired,
the complemen-
tary coloured band will remain fairly
motionless,
and
should it move away will return
to its proper position
of its own accord.

As dexterity can only be attained
by exercise,
it is a good plan to train the eyes upon
some inanimate object before proceeding
to the
examination of the human subject.

All of that came from G.

Where do we go from there?

Over to my other notebook is where.

This light poem for George Quasha
is being continued in the 1972 notebook
end of 71 & first half of 72

[The notebook to which Mac Low refers has not been located. —Eds.]

41ˢᵗ Light Poem: for Sharon Mattlin—19 June–14 July 1972

A SEQUENCE OF 31 ONE-PAGE POEMS

1

A student lamp lights the paper-and-cloth-strewn room
the large hard blue-sheeted mattress
the magazines papers & books beside & behind it
the blankets & clothes festooning the chairs
the scintillating multicolored painting *Waves*
on the wall the left side of the mattress presses
the dark blue painting across the room
beside the tree-leaved window
the unused easel the white dresser the photographs & drawings
all these nostalgic artifacts transformed
to companions of present—
of all things—happiness!
simple affection & pleasure
shared credible acceptance

the student lamp on the mess of reading matter
on the floor behind the head of the horsehair mattress
lights irrelevant images & words
as we stroke & lick & kiss each other's bodies
as our tongues & lips stroke and taste each other
in endless kisses

2

how sentimental & ordinary

that may be your response
to what I think's the hard light
of just telling the news

if this is the ordinary
let me lead an ordinary life
the rest of my life

I find that green-walled
student-lamp-lit scene
as mysterious
as awesome
& harder to believe
than an aurora borealis

no mere radiance
thrown on our embraces
by recollection
makes them seem magical
& hard to believe

do I need fantastic images
to body forth these feelings

3

my fantasies are very literal
I fantasize scenes that may well be
but I'm still filled with wonder when they happen

when we make love together
I live my fantasies

must I burn olive oil
In Aladdin's lamp
to shine a light
magical enough
into these lines
for others to share
this ordinary wonder

I have to write my poems
in natural light
or at least in artificial
full illumination

you & our being together
are not beautiful like anything else
or painted by some kind of beautiful light
but are being itself being light

4

Another day over ten days later
I'm sitting in your backyard
on 92nd St.
on 3 sides your neighbors' ailanthus trees
crowd into a shade over your backyard
tho none of them grow in it

It's like a Rousseau jungle overhead

I sit in a lawn chaise
padded with stripes of foam rubber
covered with yellow green & orange
floral-patterned pastel plastic

This ailanthus jungle overhead
is just the most wonderful thing

What was I about to say—
that I'm happy
that I'm amazed to be saying that
I'm happy

I sit here in a green easy light

5

Each page of this poem is a poem

an arbitrary structural decision
made while working on pages 2 & 3

an iridescent pigeon
like Gay Neck of my childhood book
by Dhan Gopal Mukerji
comes to the birdfeeder
not five feet in front of my feet
near the top of a fence post
Another one comes with a gayer neck
He's sitting on top of the feeder
Another's down the fence a way
perching in the sun

He just flew away

The other's gone now too

The green & purple of the pigeons' necks
gleams with a kind of luminescence—
like unexpected happiness after much sorrow

6

You love me & you let me love you
we both so want to love & be loved by
somebody we can love

It's so easy to love you

I wish I knew more ways of giving myself to you
the more I know you the more I love you

Over the ailanthus leaves
where a low-flying helicopter crosses now
the sky's grown cloudy
Thru the beautiful greys & blues
shines a creamy lucence

A darkish blue-grey profile passes overhead

The breeze freshens a bit a new pigeon appears
with lots of white spots on his head & neck
he perches on the feeder in the lessening light

Just inside the window
Clarinda watches television

7

Are you still at the table in there
correcting your typing in electric light
I can't see you from here

Putting my notebook down
I frightened another green & purple neck

I get up & go inside & find you're typing upstairs
I heat the coffee & start new water &
watch Superman awhile with Clarinda
Out in the yard there's the magic light of
just before a storm

Mordecai turns on the hose
He argues about watering a closed window
I say he shdnt because there may be cracks
He says he doesn't see any cracks
He says 'I just had an idea'
& goes into the house for something
I look up thru the Rousseau green
It's starting to rain & it's starting to thunder
M takes off his clothes & turns on the hose
'Why shd we be in all that hurry to get my underpants on?'

It's starting to rain

8

The Rousseau foliage overhead
umbrellas the rain from me for a while
but finally drops get thru
to fall on my book & arms & hair
I continue sitting in the garden chair
I brush the raindrops from my pages
I look up at the beautiful gray of the sky
between the green massings
of even-pinnate leaves
the benevolent Chinese immigrant
stubbornly perennial ailanthus
umbrellas the light rain away till it stops
so Mordecai turns the hose on himself
'I push it up & turn it on high'
a quick cooling shower   I shudder
you've come downstairs   I see you inside
'What do you want with water boiling?'

I rush inside make coffee & put on a Coltrane record
I sit at the dining table writing a lazy loving light poem
the thunder crashes
Coltrane ranges all thru his horn's range
screaming at its extremest squeak
as thunder rolls outside

9

Crashing woodpiles falling
as the rapid cymbals sizzle
Archie Shepp goes everywhere at once
hoarse as a whisky soprano
honking & screaming & travelling all over
I can hardly hear the others
now it's all bass & vibes & cymbals
now Archie's in again & the thunder too
the Museum of Natural History's
grandiloquent theme sounds over the drums
'to stem the tide of ecological suicide
the stars above'   the audience claps
'Education's in my blood   I can't quit
—Harvard wdnt sell—I shd get you Vassar'
the Addams family on TV
the thunder crashes over the phoney spookiness
"Les Matins des Noires" of Archie Shepp
with M-M & Clarinda quarreling
Now they're quietly watching the tube
& Bobby Hutcherson's vibes
quietly wanders over Joe Chambers' cymbals
& Barre Phillips' bass
as Archie sings in his tenor's extremes

10

It's the 3rd of July & I'm home
listening to romantic piano music on the radio

you've gone to your job

I made the kids & me breakfast
granola milk apple juice toast & butter
coffee for this abject addict of caffeine
& went back to bed for awhile

I've been reading & thinking about you
& feel such untempered love
such love untempered by holding back
by any holding back
such love as I'd never hoped to feel again

Where every time I touch your lips or tongue
every time I touch your clitoris
with fingertips or tongue
or lips
every time I touch you with my fingertips
every time our lips & tongues touch
I'm saying over & over & over I love you
I love you I love you I love you I love you I love you

11

We're saying over & over & over I love you
whenever our bodies & eyebeams touch
whenever we kiss or lick or stroke or pet
whenever we hug each other close
whenever your tongue & lips caress my cock
whenever my tongue & lips caress your clit
whenever my cock's in your cunt & we're fucking
we're fucking & we're smiling
O such smiling fucking
How I love your smiling fucking!
How I love our smiling fucking!
I love you Sharon & our smiling fucking

& when I hold your buttocks under you
& lick your lovely vulva till you come
while you lick & lip my penis
while you suck & tongue my penis till I come
our mouths are saying to each other's pleasure nerves
I love you   I love you

Those who've not made love
meaning at most I like you & like what you do to me
& like to do this because I like you
may laugh at these lines' obvious sentimentality
not knowing I speak of a difference
like that between the moon's light & the sun's

12

The 41st Light Poem
has taken the bit in its jaws
& turned into a sequence of short odes
following no pattern
speaking of our love as the words come to me
being direct & simple without trying
hoping I'll be believed
when I use the ordinary words
speaking of love & making love
as if we'd just discovered them
first voyagers into these magical archipelagoes
first to dive & float in these warm lagoons

Now I have no need
"to construct something
upon which to rejoice"
for I rejoice

"Although I *did* not hope to turn again
Although I *did* not hope
Although I *did* not hope to turn"
I've turned again & bless the blessèd face
the blessèd face of you with whom I've turned again to hope & to rejoicing
Sharon (Shah-róhn)'s "probably from a root
meaning 'plain' or 'level country.'"

13

Sharon (Shah-róhn)
"The undulating plain
extending from Joppa & Ramieh
northward along the Meterranean
Coast to Mt. Carmel;
about 50 m. long
and varying
from 9 to 12 m. in breadth.

The oak still flourishes in
the northern portion as probably in
the days of Isaiah;

the southern portion
is richly cultivated.

In early spring the luxuriant grass
and richly colored flowers
render this plain the garden
of Palestine.

Unfortunately,
the sand-dunes along the sea
are persistently encroaching upon it."

Oh let me help you shovel back the sand-dunes

14

Nothing desperate
I go & stop when I want
writing this poem of light
this poem of our love

These last 2 years I've learned to love
after losing love I thought forever
& we love as equals
tho you've just turned 20
& I'll be 50 in a couple months
("Soulmates," Iris said sarcastically
when you said you didn't mind the mess I make
the book & paper & toy mess that we live in
—& she probably really knew how truly she spoke)

Like our gay brothers and sisters
we (openly) love despite a deep taboo
a deeply taught & deeply learned taboo
"Younger & older must not love each other"

Solidarity
Yes that hackneyed word
Solidarity with all of you
dear lesbians & pederasts
& all the rest of you who love
those you're not supposed to love

& because we 2 seem more alike
than any 2 of the same age & sex

15

Sitting beside you in the IRT local

A black man with a knitted black scalp cap
stares at you thru spectacles
& balances on the floor beside his feet
a big mirror or a picture in a frame
with the dark blank wooden side out
the other side's covered by his raincoat
he stares & stares at you & sometimes stares at me
on his left little finger
is a thick ring gold & white from here
it's 51st St & he stares down the other way
then he stands at the door & stares at you directly
before he gets off the train at 77th

After your being threatened at Astor Place
by the red-capped black man who wanted you
just you & "his bag wasn't fucking"
who said he'd hit you & force you to come to his place
if I didn't show up by 7:30
I was uptight about this new admirer
& glad he got off at the station before our own

& then we found your parents & sisters back
& we walked all the way back to the subway
stood there tossed a quarter & did the opposite
walking again back here
where I sit on your bed & write this
while your parents sleep in the room below us

16

I sit you lie on your bed
writing in our writing books
you unclothed & lovely
I still wearing shirt pants & headband
red headband you gave me & green buttoned polo shirt
red white & blue corduroy pants
patterned like an oriental rug
You write in orange ink with an orange marking pen
with a grey lid with a white dot on its end
I look at you & we look at each other & smile
I think I'll rest this poem for awhile

Now I'm home a day & a half later
sitting in my kitchen
eating & smoking pot
drinking coffee Pernod & apple juice
none mixed with other
after eating hamburger baked in the oven
succotash & cherries
the midday meal I made for Clarinda, M-M & me
after Clarinda & I got back
from my therapy session with Chuck

I'm thinking about the difference between
loving "as a friend" & "being in love"
& being surprised all over again with the reality of the difference
I'd thought I'd never really feel again

17

Michael I loved & Michael I still love
He & I might have loved each other
as you & I do   had our bodies
drawn each other as strongly as yours & mine

Had I not fallen in love with Michael,
I'd never have known I still cd fall in love

Michael I love   you love Naomi
we love each other all the more
why "all the more"?

we love each other in the way we do
inwardness & outwardness not two

we love to touch each other
even if we're sleeping or falling asleep

from which simple touch
transition to those other ways of touching is so gradual
with such interesting names
we're half surprised to find ourselves   hovering luxuriantly
in pleasure's undemanding atmosphere
long hovering luxuriantly near climax
prolonging & enriching   varying & complicating
pleasure with endless caresses
making love saying love being love
loving to help each other come as much as coming
in loving conversation of all senses
feasting with each other till the birds begin breakfast

18

I want to write a poem
just about eating your pussy
how my heart pours love thru my tongue
when I lick your clitoris
while my hands under your ass press you toward me
not only when you glory my cock
loving it with lips & tongue & fingers

Now it's 8 days later
A huge wind just sprang up
I'm listening to high xylophones & whistlers
in Steve Reich's "Drumming"
While I was writing the first part
you called & told me about your mother's anger
"I ought to have known better"
"Known what?" asked Chuck
"Not to fall in love with a young woman?"

No I don't know my place
any better than uppity blacks
or angry dykes & faggots
who know what's gay about it & what's not
(was it 20 years ago my gay friend asked
"what's gay about it?")

I'm gay as I remember you leaving here today
in your short pink Pakistani dress with silver mirrors on it

19

You think I overpraise & overvalue
your "physical" presence
ignoring your spiritual realities

when I speak of your body I speak of the soul that informs it

(The soul must be a substance
in the
sense of
the form of a natural body
having
life potentially within...
the first grade of actuality
of a
natural organized body,"
says Aristotle's Soul-book)

I love you as the body you are
that your soul forms as time goes

I don't love you for any "traits"
"physical" or "mental"
I love you for your you-ness
Sharon, who reflect yourself
in every part of you
"inward"
"outward"
&
for
both

20

The organ on the radio plays
Bach's big prelude & fugue—in what?
I'm reading Aristotle "On the Soul," Book II,
in the Oxford translation
with wondering admiration

How came I to love this mighty mind?

No wonder a millenium believed even his mistakes
Being so often right how cd he ever be wrong?

"it
is as
meaningless to ask
whether the wax and
the shape given to
it by the
stamp are
one,"
as to ask "whether the soul and the body are one"

Oh Sharon Sharon
thank you for being you
thank you for being you with me
thank you thank you for letting me be
me with you being you with me

21

The 41st Light Poem's become
a book-length sequence of one-page poems
That never happened to me before
at least I don't think it did
& here I am in 21
& I haven't mentioned a kind of light since 7
Arc light Aurora borealis Actinic rays
Aurora australis Atom-bomb light
Artificial light Annealing-lamp light
Alcohol-lamp light Argand-lamp light
Advancing ignition Afterglow *Aufklärung*
Aureola Aureole Azure light
Aluminothermic light
Acetylene light Actinism Anda-oil lamp light
feel yourself
bathing in
whichever of these kinds of light
you want to feel yourself
bathing in

I imagine you in each of these lights in turn
Sharon in Arc light Sharon in the light of
an Aurora borealis
all right
but not Sharon in Actinic-rays or Atom Bomb Light
not Sharon oh *not* Sharon in the light of Actinism
Around Sharon's an aureole of azure light

22

"That program was live
Our next scheduled program will be the news
& that'll be at 6:30"
& then some gospel-like singing
& then you phoned

It's so good to hear you in your voice's transformations
even to hear you
over the telephone

Dear young woman whom I love
This is no hyperbole
I love you more than I can ever tell you

What do I mean by "more"?
What do I mean "than I can ever tell you"?
Isn't it my business
to be able to tell you?

It's not the more or less
It's that it goes back & forth so good
Our love for each other
I love your body & its form your soul
I love your being's actuality
I love you in action & in rest

23

Despite dear Aristotle
the qualities of soul that draw love
are not separable
Let me share the radio with you:

The Winnebago Indians ate Peyote to have children
"Whenever they held Peyote meetings we attended...
in the meeting I wd just sit there
I wd sit there all night
if I stood up everyone wd look at me
The sky was terribly black
The storm clouds came whirling
Thundered repeatedly Sky was dark
There was a mighty wind
& their clothes were blowing about them
Where are they fleeing?
There is nowhere on earth to flee to
Jesus is the only place to flee to
I stood up & raised my arm
I prayed
I was just very contented
I was an angel
I wanted to fly right away
I cd not because my time was not completed
I understand that this religion is holy"
(Mountain Wolf Woman
among the Peyotists of Nebraska
Eventually the religion gained converts
& a measure of respectability)

24

"I took care of that old lady
I bathed her & took care of her
One whole winter I took care of her
then she said
I am able to take care of myself
because I am able to use my hands"
So Mountain Wolf Woman saved an old lady
from death thru neglect

Do we praise Mountain Wolf Woman
because she saved a poor old lady
by taking care of her & loving her

In April of 1936
Mountain Wolf Woman's husband died
"Maybe this never happened to me
The worse thing was when my man died
Your husband had double pneumonia
& tuberculosis—that's what your husband died of
They took the whole house apart
They stacked the boards
They rebuilt the house for her on gov't land
Whatever the white people say
That is the way it has to be
Her daughter married a conscientious objector
who was sent to do work in Oregon"

Mother women too work There we got paid
on Friday We used carriers that hold 3 quarts
Each carrier paid $1.50 ($2.50?)
I went to where we were picking
I cried as loud as I cd
When I cried myself out I stopped
She wd jump in the air
Mother Mother brother sent a letter
He was safe in the Second World War
They were wearing khaki uniforms
The boy across from me got up
"Now I have a mother
He was glad he said because now he had a letter"
Your daughter left your children
because of your husband
She wrote me a letter
She went through this misfortune
There were a lot of fruit trees
Their eyes filled with tears
We will be going home
They stayed with me & grew big
I had 11 children & they were born here & there
38 grandchildren 9 great grandchildren
I go visiting here & there
His adopted daughter   a white girl
Auntie, she said—we will write down these stories in a book

26

People who are old & wise & good
are privileged to know the time of their own deaths

"Whatever is good, that I wd do
Whatever is good to say, that I wd say
I always ask of him
That I move in a good way
where I live I care for myself
I say I am happy
I expect to go to heaven
I say no more"

So Mountain Wolf Woman died in peace

Let McGovern govern & Eagleton fly
I'll be a reformist till the day I die

I just heard their acceptance speeches
"capitalist politicians" Oh yes sure but
Oh what a relief to hear *those* voices for awhile
rather than trying-to-keep-a-straight-face Nixon
& utterly sincere & evil Agnew
or the jittery-liberal whine of Hubert Humphrey

"I'll stop the bombing of Indo-China
on the day I'm inaugurated
& get all troops & prisoners back & out
in ninety days"

So spake McGovern

27

Sitting in the kitchen
writing poetry
trying to reconcile
the honest sound of McGovern's voice
& the good things he promises explicitly
with his helping to cause the defeat
of all the minority planks
those to enforce the human rights of gays
to let women control their own wombs
to legalize this gentle female hemp
to guarantee to each family of 4
a minimum income of $6,500
McGovern defeated them all
He had a working majority all the way thru

The theory is:
Trust the man to do what he can't say he'll do & win

I nearly believe it when I hear that voice
So much of the person & his own energy coming thru
Not trying to keep a straight face He laughs
He likes to laugh He feels good being the winner
He's going to make damn sure he'll be the Big Winner

Just help me win that giggle signals
& I'll do my damnest to help you

I think most of us wd breathe a little easier
but as for the overthrow of capitalism
that'll have to wait a while longer

28

Delirium of love speech
my tongue on your vulva's
petals and pistil

My words tumble over each other on those lips
while your mouth whispers love songs on my penis

I'm so grateful to all those friendly spirits
(It's not for nothing they're all named like saints
Paul & Michael & Jerome   & Diane & Armand)
who helped bring us together
who made it possible for both of us
to speak love's language meaning love

I love your body I love you in & thru your body
Oh yes the inward I loves the inward you
& loves the outward you the inward spun

The hunger you assuage   The need you feed
is more than need for pleasure or beauty
I never realized I still had such a need
to love & be loved all the way all the way all the way
to love & be loved every way all the way
to be loved & to love every way in every way

It's so hard really to speak of love & not be mushy
It's so hard to say just the way it is

Cocteau writes of someone's "falling into heaven"
falling in love *is* falling into heaven
where the light of Truth flooding us
reveals each other's infinite worth

29

But why can't we always see
everyone's infinite worth
Why must we fall in love
fully to experience another person's value
another person's being
falling in love's pulling back a curtain
or at least a corner of a curtain
the enlightened person feels this way
about everyone & everything
Satori's falling in love with all the world

Sharon reality shines thru you & is you
Truth shines from your eyes even when you're anxious
Your inward light shines I speak to it
I can speak to your most inward light
with words with caresses with my eyes

The sky's getting light   I sit here writing
I keep trying to say I love you & what it's like
to love you & be loved by you
A natural azure light fills the kitchen window top
I turn off the bulb to see it better   To see

I write quickly as the sky grows lighter
I want to go back & lie beside you as you sleep
I want to see your face when you wake
I want to smile at you & see you smile
I want to stroke you & be stroked by you
I want to kiss you & be kissed by you

30

Sometimes I don't think I deserve you
Sometimes I hardly think I deserve you
Sometimes I think I deserve you
Sometimes I know it's just the *I* I am
that *can* deserve you
Sometimes I know we really deserve each other
& sometimes I know there's no deserving love
or not deserving it

Falling in love is something we do & that happens
We do it as we fall into water or heaven
We bring ourselves to the brink
Then if it happens it happens

We deserve it as we deserve being heavy enough
to fall
when we bring ourselves to the brink
where we *may* fall

After that there's no deserving or not deserving

Love's no respecter of persons
Love's the only respecter of persons

But all our lives
we've been taught
we must come to deserve love
that we'll be rewarded with love
for living up to criteria
for following others' rules of right behavior

not for falling into the sky

31

I'm waiting in the 163ʳᵈ St IND station
waiting for a train to take me to you
to where you may already be waiting
at Dyckman St & Broadway

Have they turned off the subway for the night?
I seem to have been here an hour
I don't want to be late to meet you
I'm sure I'll be late now
even tho the train's here now

I'll still have to change to an A train
since this AA only goes to 168ᵗʰ St

Now I'm waiting at 168ᵗʰ St for an A
I don't like your having to wait
because of your recent scare
the man who threatened to make you go with him
when you were waiting for us at Astor Place

My watch says 16 minutes after 9
I said I'd be at that corner by 9
The train that terminated here is roaring
I keep seeming to hear an A approaching

The AA moves out of the station going uptown
no passengers or lights on it
Another AA arrives & one's parked across the track
People keep arriving
the 2ⁿᵈ AA pulls out empty
The A train's arriving

42ⁿᵈ Light Poem: *In Memoriam* Paul Goodman—
Midnight 21 August–2:46 AM 22 August 1972

Perennial light! rising again & again
light in the darkness of our bully's-war time
antagonistic light
combatting evil on all sides
till friends you fought as foes
& anger broke your heart
& tore you from us all
friends
& enemies
& friends you took for enemies

Angry angry Paul
Friendly angry Paul
Friendly spiteful Paul
Paul who warned us long ago
more to heed your words
than your deeds
tho often your actions
lived those careful words

You United-Statesian light
that only cdve come to be
in this time & this place
loving & hating your country & your time
scolding & caressing
you loving loving light
you patriotic Paul
anarchistic Paul
utopian conservative
antimoral moralistic Paul

2

How can we believe youre gone
How can we believe
your unexpected voice & hand
will never again give us new surprises
never again forbid us

247

easy acceptance of your thoughts
or of what we thought you thought

You loved peripety
the probable reversal
the turnaround seemingly unexpected
yet utterly prepared for

You never let well enough alone
even though you praised & sought
the *tolerable* society
for you knew well enough
was never good enough
& you gave good light

How you must have alienated
lazy-minded student audiences
never letting them settle back
in passive Oh-wow acceptance
or dreamy dropout ease

Always against the grain
always espousing the unacceptable
sex in Academia
professionalism amid the sexy rebels

Cantankerousness was your cause
not your middle name
Socratic cantankerousness
probably seeking rejection
& angry when you got it
gadfly in spite of yourself
forever refining your difficult lucid wisdom
leaving trails of indignant former followers

3

Against the grain
opposed to the fashions
flaunting Wordsworth when the norm was Donne
(or Eliot or Pound)

Beethoven when Bach & Mozart reigned
Satie in the realm of Stravinsky
Cocteau when Valéry & St.-John Perse were "in"

You even quoted William Cullen Bryant!
& rightly praised *The Song of Hiawatha*

When "everyone" hated Wagner
you centered a section of *The Grand Piano*
around *Die Meistersinger*

Long before Old Possum
gave his later proMiltonic speeches
rousing Ezra's wrath
you praised the greatest Puritan unstintingly
& never ceased to do so

You always looked at men & things
in your *own* light
& you rather liked it
when you were called old-fashioned

More & more you were coming to be
the old-fashioned light of the ages

4

But always a dark light
burned behind your cheerfulness
as when you envisioned
peeling back the sunlit scene
the sunlit scene
peeling itself back
revealing the Nothing

When Matty died on the mountain
I think part of the sunlit scene
peeled itself back
permanently

5

Manifold light
peering into every act & thought of Man
Humanisitic Paul
Paul the Man of Letters
Professional whose province
was every human enterprise

Now they'll miss you!

All those facile specialists
who scorned you as a dabbler in their fields
& lived to use your thoughts
when you'd passed well beyond them!

6

It's often been an agonizing light
you've thrown on my own life
How often I've measured myself by you
& felt I've thrown my life away!

How often I've thought
when I've spent the day in idle reading
& getting high on pot
& the best thing I've done
is play a bit with the children:
"Paul is probably writing
& studying & thinking
Paul is probably preparing
irritating surprises
for his myriad facile disciples

"He's probably discovering
brand-new ways to look at things
or rediscovering ancient ones
everyone's scorned for granted"

& yet your deepest teaching
was how I must live myself
how I must have faith

that even my idleness
is part of my way & work

That Character
is Destiny

7

No more new light from Paul
you've given us all you cd

Your poems still sing to us
your critical thoughts still probe

The books are at an end
we'll have no more from you

The letters to the editors
will no more lash & sting

No more fields of knowledge
need fear your fertile harrow

You've written the last of your poems
your poems that sing themselves

I sit in the rocking chair writing about you Paul
while Sharon lies asleep nearby

"Now go to her," I hear you say
& see your lovely smile.

43rd Light Poem: 2nd for Sharon Mattlin—19 November 1972

Sharon let me tell you
all the kinds of light
I love you in:

In sunlight
In starlight
In St. Elmo's Fire

In the spectrum
In sodium-vapor-lamp light
In sapphire light

In shimmering light
In shaded light
In shimmer

In streetlamp light
In sunshine
In shining light

In safety-lamp light
In Saturn light
In shade

In shadowy light
In shadowed light
In St. Germain-lamp light

In student-lamp light
In smoking-lamp light
In solar light

In spotlight light
In sunstone light
In seal-oil-lamp light

In supernova light
In scintillance
In sheen

In sparkling
In a sparkle
In a scintilla

In stoplight light
In sunrise
In shine

In a sunset
In a sunbeam
In spark-igniter light

In a spark

In happy light
In heraldic light
In heavenly light

In holy light
In heavy light
In heartlight

In hot light
In high light
In a highlight

In a hankering light
In a hungering light
In a hungry light

In half light
In hospitable light
In honey light

In a heady light
In headlight light
In head light

In a habile light
In habitual light
In Hadean light

In harmonious light
In hallucinatory light
In hairy light

In hairlight
In hakam light
In a halcyon light

In a hymning light
In hymnlight
In Himmel

In hemplight
In a hempen light
In a hemispheral light

In a hemispherical light

In a heterogeneous light
In a heterosexual light
In a heterotelic light

In arclight light
In aurora borealis light
In afterglow

In an aureole
In an aureola
In an aurora

In aurora australis light
In artificial light
In amethyst light

In azure light

In amber light

In acetylene light

In an absolute light

In an accepting light
In actual light

In an affectionate light

In angry light
In accidental light

In ambitious light
In asparagus light
In accurate light

In arrogant light
In arrant light
In airy light

In the light of the ages

In aching light

In aimless light

In an ambidextrous light
In an ambisexual light
In ambient light

In ambiguous light
In ambisinister light
In ambivalent light

In archaic light

In arcane light

In architectural light
In architectonic light
In archetypal light

In almond-oil-lamp light

In amazing light

In amusing light
In Ariel light

In real light
In radiance
In radiant light

In reflected light
In rainbow light
In red light

In radiation

In rays of light
In refulgence
In resplendence

In rose light
In rose lamplight
In a rosy light

In a reading light
In a reading-lamp light

In ragged light
In raging light
In rain light

In rapid light
In rapturous light
In recaptured light

In a reaching light

In a repeating light
In repeated light

In ruby light
In Rubicon light
In a rueful light

In a revolving light

In a rollicking light

In rock light
In a rocking light

In rocket light
In rocketing light
In rickety light

In riotous light

In ripe light

In a ribald light
In rippling light

In owllight
In orange light
In old light

In outdoor light
In outdoor firelight
In orgone

In orgone radiation

In orgone lumination

In outrageous light
In oil-lamp light
In oily light

In ontological light
In odd light

In ostrich light

In overreaching light
In overarching light

In ovarian light

In osprey light
In operant light
In opulent light

In observant light
In observing light
In observatory light

In ocular light
In oscular light

In osculatory light
In oscillating light
In an obscure light

In an open light

In an oval light

In oatlight
In oaklight
In ōmlight

In ozone light

In Ozlight
In orchestral light
In orchid light

In new light
In nude light
In numinous light

In noonlight

In noontide light
In naked light
In nova light

In noonday light
In natural light

In needed light
In night light
In night-light light

In Neptune light

In a north light
In northern lights

In neon light
In a nimbus
In nickelodeon light

In neat light
In a neat light

In nebular light
In nebulous light
In a nebula's light

In negative light
In nebulescent light
In nebuliferous light

In necessary light

In necromantic light
In nonnecromantic light
In a nervous light

In nervelight

In novel light
In naval light
In navel light

In nameless light
In a naming light
In named light

44th Light Poem: 3rd one for Sharon Mattlin—25 November 1972

Sharon the light that streams
from
your face when we meet

changes my life feeling
brings
me suddenly home

to the light of your eyes
whose
light leads to feedback

as eyes reflect eyelight
souls
resonate in love

love reflects love reflects
love
love reflecting love

generating feedback

45th Light Poem: 4th one for Sharon Mattlin—25 November 1972

Sharon soul 'n' body
you
soul-body Sharon

light mine light treasury
dear
light I hunger for

whenever you're away
face
I move towards in dreams

I open towards in life
soul
I move & open towards

what kind of light is this
light
lovelight or lustlight

what if it's lifelight

46th Light Poem: 5th one for Sharon Mattlin—25 November 1972

Sharon's Light Poem Odes
Yours
Let me give you these

This is what I can make
bring
as other men bring

bracelets pendants earrings
rings
solid words of love

no I don't call them jewels
you kindle light & words

the words knit together
here
you must see the light

shimmer thru my stammer

47th Light Poem: For Sharon Belle Mattlin—28 January–4 February 1974

A special light illumines the beginning.

Is it an honorific light?
It is certainly in your honor
& in honor of our love
& is a helping light
an ameliorating light
for the anguish of the absence of your light
between our times together.

It is a reaffirming light—
a light wherein our love is reaffirmed.
It is a real light.

Kisses in a red light of a concert
on the floor on the floor below the kitchen
as Charlemagne's piano
plays responses to our energies
as Charlemagne the puppet moves his hands

That my darling was several days ago
Now it's nearly 3 in the morning
of the 4th of February 1974.
I'm going to fly to Chicago in a few hours

The memory of your voice
The vision of your face
The feeling of my lips & tongue
as they moved beyond my will
over your labia
over your clitoris
over the mouth of your vagina

The joy and excitement
of giving you this pleasure
directly with the mouth
that kisses you & says, "Sharon, I love you!"
mounts & mounts till my mouth glows
& I nearly come

I hover at orgasm edge
(but never quite fall over it)
While tongue traces pleasure
over clitoris & cunt
over your smooth fragile labial folds
tenderly—abandonedly
—my mouth feeding pleasure to your mouth till you come

48th Light Poem: 2nd Light Poem for Rochelle Owens—3 August 1975

"It is not possible to contract for a stay."

Armand's voice stops & the crowd claps.
I turn the radio off & begin this poem.
I wonder how Rochelle became radioactive.
I turn the radio on again & hear static & Something-Too-Thick-For-Webern.
The oblique light of 4 PM thru southwest windows & massed house plants
& the multicolored scattered sheets from 2 copies of the mimeo'd Pronouns
& Armand & my issue of vort's red cover
& the paperback 22 Light Poems' orange cover
& the lavender 2nd bookjacket on a copy of Stanzas for Iris Lezak
& the blue & grey & black of an Ian Tyson 1970 graphic
& the red & orange & black of the Loka cover
combine to make a kind of opalescent light here in the living room at Popham Avenue.

I turned the radio off to hear the Ruth Crawford string quartet.
What do I mean I turned the radio off I mean I turned this electric typewriter off.
It makes static on the FM radio which is now playing thru the mono amplifier system.
I turned it off again to hear part of Stravinsky's 3 pieces for string quartet.
I'm going to turn it off again to hear some more.

I turn this on to write that the Light Fantastic String Quartet is about to play
Bela Bartok's 6th String Quartet:

> (the raderhearerreaderwhoever comes to this
> is aksed hear to experience Bartok's 6th
> (in its entirety))

> (I turn this staticmaker off again.)

    We interrupt this string quartet to announce that the heat wave's open fire
hydrants has lowered to water pressure so much that the toilets won't flush &
the cat shit is floating in the toilet now in the little bathroom what next?

Heatwavetyping Lnaguage: interript means interrupt has lowered to means have lowered the
Lnaguage means Language (God rest Jack Spicer).

I'ved switched from WBAI to WQXR to hear the 5 o'clock news with static who cares?
President Ford is in Yugoslavia with President Tito

& a plane full of Moroccans crashed in an Atlas Mountain intto an Atlas Mountain
& it was 103 degrees at street level at Rockerfeller Center & there's a water emergency
& there's a mounting fire danger as the water's reduced to a trickle in some areas
about 5,000 people slept on the beaches last night continued hot & humid tomorrow
tomorrow very hote & humid with a chance of thunfershowers tundershowers oi my roofless
(hote means hot thungerfowers means thunfershower means tundershowqers means
tundershowers means thundershowers thundershowers thundershowers
thundershowers thundershowers thundershowers oi my roofless loft down on North
Moore Street (dja hear, Rochlee (Rochlee means Rochelle) I"m we're moving from
Popham Avenue Bronx to 42 North Moore Street New York New York 10013—you &
George must come to dinner as soon as we're "properly settled in" (by later September I
hi not hi ho hope I hope by later Sept.).

The radio's been off a while since the end of the 5 o'clock QXR neas means news.
Oh oh the radio in the kitchen's still drooling on I think it's still on BAI .
I'll turn this off to go on means in to turn that off.

"He didn't even recognize it when he conducted it."
Mahler as shaman he means Mahlet means Mahler it means his 3ʳᵈ Symphony
Mahler didn't know his own or "own" 3ʳᵈ Symphony it was given him so completely
but sometimes he might not know it when another conductor conducts it no names please.

Woman talking on BAI anout means about conductors & virtuosi going into trance states
during performances there is now way any performer can be the cinposer completely
means "There is no way any performer can be the performer completely…. There's no
way one can hear exactly as a composer hears. But the state of consciousness the
composer sought to induce … what does one do? What does this person seek? What
was his era like? Nietzsche & Wagener means Wagner as much as she dislikes them are
part of Mahler's fabric—part of his background…" M-M just got in.

Talking of music: "One time's shamanism is not that of another."

Mayor Beame appeals to citizens to use as little ater as possible ater means water.
"Cloudy very warm & humid … the high in the low 90's … right now o0 means 90 degrees
…FBI Agens today interviewed the family of … James Hoffa … missing … 148
passengers killed in Moroccan mountains plane crash …"

I turn off the radio again & get back to this Light Poem & wonder at the kind oo means
of Light Poem this Light Poem seems to be becoming.

~~Somewhere around the middle of the Bartok it occurred to me that this might be a kind~~

of Action Poetry in Rosenberg's sense of Action Painting but not Spontaneous Bop
Prosody in Allen's sense at all. E.g., you leave in some of the typing mistakes
others you correct or x out.

Leave it to you Rochelle Owens to turn my light means Light Poems in a new direction.

Mordecai-Mark is going to Maine in a few hours. The Carsons with whom Clarinda's
been staying a week or two & with whom M-M's gnna be staying most of the rest of August
came down to New York to take Jack Carson"s means Carson's German daughters & one of the
German daugher means daughters' boy friends & a friend of her boy friend to
the airport on the way back to Germany Amin wanted to bomb Dar-es-salaam & the Israelis
wdnt help him with air½ neans means with airplanes & sophisticated weapons "The
man's not mature in mental viewpoint," says an Israeli diplomat.

It's nearly 10 to 7 PM Sunday 3 August 1975.
It's 96 degrees Fahrenheit here in the living room whre means where I'm typing.
M-M's doing his packing to go to Maine & as much of his room as possible before he goes.
I'll need him here some more in the last week of August when we move or thereabouts
but I want him to get up to the country & get some clean air & exercise for about 3
weeks so he'd better go to Maine tonight when there's a ride going up with the Carsons
means the Carsons are going up & can take him up with them rather than his having to
take the bus & stay on the bus a long time & change at Lewiston & pay a lot of bus fare.
How is all this getting into this Light Poem?

There's nothing opalescent about the light in the living room now
but I've intermittently been imagining Rochelle declaiming in the light of a cresset
by the light of a cresset in the light by the light in the light shed by a cresset
("an iron vessel for holding an illuminant, as burning oil or pitchy wood, and
mounted as a torch, or hung as a lantern").

I imagine a cresset hunf hunf means hung hung below a crennellation
at the top of a tower on which behind the crennellation stands Rochelle.
The light from the cresset fitfully hyperdramatically lights Rochelle declaiming
proclaiming exclaiming screaming complaining plaining.

M-M just left for Maine with Jack Carson it's 9:10 PM in the Bronx just the cats & me.

Just me & the cats & the plants I just took a shower it's not quite 100 degrees here.

Oh Rochelle's the one to be keening her poems in the light shed by a cresset as she
stands on the top of a tower her face & upper figure visible behind a crenel
the pary pary means parts the parts that stick up are the merlons the parts that are

open places are the embrasures or crenels.

The cresset is hung on the outside of the tower on a large hook just below the crenel behind which Rochelle stands with her red hair streaming in the wind & the cresset's black smoke she is singing Rochelle is singing her untutored intensity makes my hair stand on end I'm watching from not far away not far below I must be on another tower or a high window somewhere else in the castle or fortress is Rochelle the defending Countess or the triumphant Revolutionary Leader of the Peasants & Workers how she sings!

I must be at a high window or on a slightly lower wall or tower I can hear her keening for all on both sides lost so far during the siege.

Is she the Countess who is the Revolutionary Leader of the Workers & Peasants defending her castle fortress against tt the furious forces of Reaction?

During the coming month I'll have to pack everything up that's not packed yet & move it all from here in the Bronx to North Moore Street.

It's probably *North* Moore Street because there's another Moore Street farther south down by the Battery when I said "down by the Battery" someone either M-M or Brian or myabe it was Sharon envisioned a hughe means huge storage battery down at the south end of Manhattan near which is the other Moore Street.

& amybe means maybe.

Now this is the way I got St. Elmo's Fire for Rochelle's H:
I; I've been using a variation of the method used in composing Jerry Rothenberg's Light Poem (the 27th: see Vort #8, p. 34) & so's not to get the same light names I've been crisscrossing:
R is the 18th letter of the al½habet & R-18 on the chart is refracted light as in Jerry's Light Poem & O is the 15th letter & O–15 is amazonstone light as in Jee Jee means Jerry's LPbut "crisscross" & you get R-15 radioactivity ("I wonder how Rochelle became radioactive." & there she had just been active on the radio) & you get O–18 opalescent light & then you crisscross C–3 with H–8 & you get C–8 cresset light & H–3 which is pretty near S–3 (H sounds a little like S) since there ain't no H's in the lists from the chart (I can"t find the chart tho I'm almost certain I had it when I unpacked from Engalnd by by means but I can"t find it so I'm having to use the lists from the charts charts means chart given at the back of 22 Light Poems) so here I come to S–3 St. Elmo"s Fire.

"ST. ELMO'S FIRE, the glow accompanying the brushlike discharges of atmospheric electricity which usually appears as a tip of light on the extremities of pointed objects such a church towers or the masts of ships during stormy weather.

It is commonly accompanied by a crackling or fizzing noise.

"St. Elmo's fire, or corona discharge, is commonly observed on the periphery of
propellers, along the wing tips, wins means windshield and nose of aircraft flying
in dry snow, ice crystals or in the vicinity of thunderstorms. The discharge may
be sufficiently strong to cause a noisy disturbance in the radio, called static,
which may obliterate all other signals. The corona discharge from an aircraft may
initiate a lightning discharge which, striking the aeroplane, may cause small
structural damage, impair the radio or temporarily blind the pilot. Various flight
procedures, in addition to mechanical and electrical devices designed to reduce
the charge accumulation, are utilized as safeguat safe guat means safeguards
are utilized as safeguards in preventing or minimizing discharges.
The name St. Elmo is an Italian corruption, through *Sant' Ermo*, of St. Erasmus,
the patron saint of Mediterranean sailors, who regard St. Elmo's fire as the
visible sign of his guardianship."

Encyclopedia Britannica, V. 19, p. 828, Chicago, 1957.

The EB provides elucidation of St. Elmo's fire except that they don't tell its color.
I can imagine St. Elmo's fre as a flickering lemon-colored light acompn accompn means
accompanied means "accompanied by a crackling or fizzing noise."

The cresset has burned itself out.
Rochelle's still standing on the tower, but now in silence.
A lightning storm's coming up & already the merlons are outlines against the black
cloud-filled sky brightened by occasional distant lightning
by flashes of lemon-colored St. Elmo's fire lemon St. Elmo's fire flickering on the
tops of the merlons on each side of Countess Rochelle Leader of the People.
Long ago she divided secretly her vast domain among the myriad peasants & artisans
living & working on it, reserving only her own apartments in the castle & that part
of her library not already given to the People's School in which she teaches.
Knowing the temperament of neighboring nobles,
she's sworn her people & all visitors to secrecy.
She dare not let it be known she;s practicing communism....
They know it won't be confined to her domain
that is, they'd know it wdnt, they know it won't.
That's why they're attacking her castle.
They know their people won't stand for the old feudal ways
while the people in the Countess Rochelle's domain are practicing anarchic communism.
They know (they wdve known & then they did know)

that they'd never fare as well at the hands of their own villeins
as the just & benevolent beautiful Countess Rochelle
whose red hair & black eyebrows proclaim communist anarchism.
(The real Rochelle's intensely a Zionist thus no anarchist
an opponent of Karl Marx but not thus necessarily no communist
but I don't know what politics moves her now except Zionism
& Marx's own hatred of exploiters & oppressorsincluding"marxist"oppressors & exploiters.)

Back tot tot be tot means death tot means to
back to the battlements.

In the lemon light of the St. Elmo's fire on the merlons of Rochelle's tower
we mix elucidation of Rochelle's politics with that of Countess Rochelle.
All this stuff about "lemon St. Elmo's Fire"'s nonsense:
"ST. ELMO'S FIRE: the bluish electrical glow sometimes seen at the tips of masts and spars
of sailing ships before and during an electrical storm. Clouds of the storm carry a
heavy charge of static electricity which attracts unlike charges on the ground. The
static electricity on the ground, attracted by the cloud charge, discharges through
pointed objects. When this point-discharge is visible, it is called St. Elmo's Fire. The
phenomenon is not exhibited by steel ships, because those are grounded; but it can
sometimes be seen on the wing tips and propellers of an airplane flying in or near a
thunderstorm. The phenomenon is named after the patron saint of Mediterranean
sailors."

The Harper Encyclopedia of Science, p. 1035, Washington, 1967.

So it's bluish & not lemon's hue.
What more elucidation do we need?

Let me really imagine a room or a space filled with opalescent light:
it's very pleasant.
I imagine being within a sphere painted white on the inside & on this white inner surface
of a sphere & within all the space contained within it
there shines a slowly changing opalescent light all is suffused with it a slowly changing
opalescent light
which momently disappears to be replaced by an intense but not quite painfully so
white light.
This new light
alternates irregularly with the opalescent light.
What is this new situation?
We're somehow comfortably within a sphere suffused alternately with opalescent light

& white light.
The old light & the new light alternate at random intervals.

Outside
there's bluish St. Elmo's Fire on the tip of the street-lamp-light's
what the hell's the right word—streetlight's?
top
but only those who look hard or see it from windows above can see it at all
so bright is the streetlight itself.

Oh Countess Rochelle Countess Rochelle we saw you for such a short time
that we can nearly believe that that's you at the foot of the streetlight.

No
you're standing in silent triumph on your tower.
You've persuaded the neib means neighboring nobles' peasant-soldiers to march away.
They're marching back to the neighboring nobles' domains with designs in their hearts.
Little reck they the power of king & pope.
Anarchist communism triumphs in this green & pleasant land
& King means king & pope be damned
they sing
king & pope be damned.

The 49ᵗʰ Light Poem: *In Memoriam* Gustav Mahler—11–12 September–3 October 1975

There is a green light shining.

It is the massed reflections of leaves & stems
of the jungle of plants growing to the right of the place of this writing
across the three living-room windows
between them & this typewriter,
this chair,
& the grand piano behind it
with ivory & ebony
keyboard nearest the stunted trees:
pushing aside an avocado branch,
the player sits with green to the right,
green between back & window:
is it this vegetal green?

Or is it the green light
that shines on the fifth day of the bardo,
"the purified element of air,"
wherein "Blessed Amoghasiddhi, lord of the circle," appears,
"his body . . . green in colour,"
holding "a double vajra in his hand,"
sitting "on a throne of shang-shang birds soaring in the sky,
embracing his consort Samaya-Tārā,"
appears "from the green northern Realm,
Accumulated Actions."?

Blessed Amoghasiddhi,
green, with a double vajra,
on a throne of shang-shang birds,
embracing Samaya-Tārā.

"The green
light
of the skandha of concept
in its basic purity,
the action-accomplishing wisdom,
brilliant green,
luminous

and clear,
sharp
and terrifying,
adorned with discs of light
will come
from the heart of Amoghasiddhi and his consort
and pierce
your
heart
so that your eyes
cannot bear to look at it.

"Do not be afraid of it.

"It is the spontaneous play of your own mind,
so rest
in the supreme state
free from activity and care,
in which there is no near
or far,
love
or hate.

"At the same time,
together with the wisdom light,
the soft
red
light of the jealous gods, caused by envy,
will also shine on you.

"Meditate so
that there is no difference between
love and hate.

"But if your intelligence is weak,
then
simply
do not take pleasure in it.

"At that time, under the influence of
intense envy,

you will be terrified
and escape
from the sharp, brilliant green light,
but you will feel pleasure
and attraction
toward the soft red light of the jealous gods.

"At that
moment
do not be afraid of the green light,
sharp
and brilliant,
luminous and clear,
but recognize it
as wisdom.

Let your mind
rest in it,
relaxed,
in a state of non-action,
and
supplicate It with devotion, thinking,
'it is the light-ray of Blessed Amoghasiddhi's compassion,
I take refuge in it.'

"It is the light-ray hook
of Blessed Amoghasiddhi's
compassion,
called
the action-accomplishing wisdom,
so
long for it
and do not escape.

"Even if you escape
it will stay with you
inseparably.

"Do not be afraid of it,
do not be attracted
to the soft

red
light of the jealous gods.

"That is the inviting path
of karma
accumulated by
your intense
envy.

"If you are attracted to it you will
fall
into the realm of the jealous gods,
and experience unbearable misery
from fighting
and quarreling.

"It is an obstacle blocking the path of liberation,
so do not
be attracted to it, but
give up your unconscious tendencies.

"Feel longing
for the luminous,
brilliant
green light,
and say this inspiration-prayer
with intense
one-
pointed concentration on
Blessed Amoghasiddhi and his consort:

"When through intense envy
I wander in saṃsāra,
on the luminous light-path
of action-accomplishing wisdom,
may Blessed Amoghasiddhi go
before me,
his consort Samaya-Tārā
behind me;
help me
to cross

the bardo's dangerous pathway
and bring me
to the perfect
buddha state."

"By saying this inspiration prayer with deep devotion,"
(you)
"will dissolve into rainbow light
in the heart
of Blessed Amoghasiddhi and his consort,
and become a sambhogakāya buddha
in the northern Realm,
Perfected Actions."

So The Great Liberation
Through Hearing In The Bardo :
Fremantle & Trungpa's English
set to another music.

Set to another music, Gustav,
it is the end of the 1st movement of your 5th,
a pizzicatto doubled C♯–G♯
that cd be C♯Major
but's "really"
C♯
minor, as we've known all along
(the 2nd movement makes that clear enough).

The green light of the "G" of Gustav shines
from the heart of the Blessed Amoghasiddhi,
who with all powers accomplishes all actions:
he sees the situation from all sides
& all that might be done
& sees what must be done
& does it;
his "crossed vajra represents,"
writes Trungpa Rinpoche,
"the area of all
activities
completely perceived
in all directions";

& he's sitting on a shang-shang bird,
a cymbal-playing garuda,
"half-human,
half eagle":
"the yogin's confidence & power":
"devours
the serpents
of poisonous
emotions":
flying thru space with Blessed Amoghasiddhi on his back
from whose heart shines terrifying bright green light:
DO NOT BE AFRAID
DO NOT ESCAPE
TAKE REFUGE IN IT
TAKE REFUGE IN THIS PIERCING GREEN LIGHT
("the light-
ray hook
of Blessed Amoghasiddhi's
compassion, called
action-accomplishing wisdom")
DO NOT BE AFRAID
LONG FOR THIS PIERCING GREEN LIGHT
LONG FOR IT
DO NOT ESCAPE
("Even if you escape
it will stay with you
inseparably.")
& the shang-shang bird clangs his cymbals:
shang-shang
SHANG-SHANG
as you dissolve into rainbow light in the heart of the Blessed Amoghasiddhi
SHANG-SHANG
& the heart of Samaya-Tārā
(shang-shang)
"the Savior of Sacred Word"
SHANG-
"or Samaya"
SHANG
("the sacred vow that binds the yogin to his
(shang-
shang)
practice").

/Gazelle./

        Samaya-Tārā

                                      /size of the
Roebuck/

        green

              /CAMEL/

                                              cymbals
/obtained/

Gus gave the green light.

Autobiography:
This has to do with my first encounter with the Green Tara
It is dedicated to the Very Venerable Kalu Rinpoche
    with whom I took refuge
                     a little over a year ago
  in the Lamas, the Yidams, the Buddha, the Dharma, the Sangha, & the Dakinis
         & other protetctors & fierce benificences
    & who then initiated me into the meditation on Chenrayzee
                              AUM MANI PADME HUM!
         AUM MANI PAYME HOONG!!
            aum mani padme hum aum mani padme hum aum mani padm
    & with whome I took my Boddhisattva vows
                     early last spring
      & lay vows abjuring killing, lying, & stealing
& who initiated me
      then, last spring

into the Vajrasattva meditation
as well as that on the Green Tara:
OM TARE TUTTARE TURE SWAHA!

om tare tuttare ture swaha om tare tuttare
ture swaha om tare tuttare ture swaha om tare tuttare ture swaha om tare tuttare ture
swaha om tare tuttare ture swaha om tare tuttare ture swaha om tare tuttare ture swaha
(this is also dedicated
to Chögyam Trungpa, Rinpoche
whose talks, books, schools, & students led me back into sitting & thence into
taking refuge
this is also dedicated to Tarthang Tulku, Rinpoche
whose fervor in preaching Dharma
teaching Dharma with flashing eyes & smiles
is a contagious health)
OM AH HUM VAJRA GURU PADMA SIDDHI HUM!
OM AH HOONG VAJRA GURU PAYMA SIDDHI HOONG!
OM AH HUM VAJRA GURU PADMA SIDDHI HUM
om ah hum vajra guru padma siddhi hum om ah hum vajra guru padma siddhi hum om ah hum
vajra guru padma siddhi hum om ah hum vajra guru padma siddhi hum om ah hum vajra guru
Padma siddhi hum om ah hum vajra guru padma siddhi hum om ah hum vajra guru padma sid
dhi hum om ah hum vajra guru padma siddhi hum om ah hum vajra guru padma siddhi hum o
m ah hum vajra guru padma siddhi hum om ah hum vajra guru padma siddhi hum om ah hum
vajra guru padma siddhi hum om ah hum vajra guru padma siddhi hum om ah hum vajra gur
u padma siddhi hum om ah hum vajra guru padma siddhi hum om ah hum vajra guru padma
siddhi hum om ah hum vajra guru padma siddhi hum om ah hum vajra guru padma siddhi hum
OM AH HOONG VAJRA GOOROO PAYMA SIDDHIE HOONG om ah hum vja vajra
vajra guru payma siddhi hoong om ah hum vajra guru padma siddhi hum om ah hum vajra gu
ru padma siddhi hum om ah vajra guru padma siddhi hum aum ah hoong vajra guru pay
ma siddhee hoong om ah hum vajra guru padma siddhi hum om ah hoong vajra gooroo payma
siddhi hoong om ah hum vajra guru padma siddhi hum om ah hum vajra guru padma siddhi
hum
aum mani payme hoong om mani padme hum aum mani payme hoong om mani padme hum om
mani payme hoong aum mani padme hum aum mani padme hum aum mani padme hum om mani pad
me hum aum mani padme hum aum mani padme hum aum mani padme hum aum mani padme hum

om tare tuttare ture swaha om tare tuttare ture swaha om tare tuttare ture
swaha om tare tuttare ture swaha om tare tuttare ture swaha om tare tuttare ture swah
a om tare tuttare ture swaha om tare tuttare ture swaha om tare tuttare ture swaha
om tare tuttare ture swaha om tare tuttare ture swaha om tare tuttare ture swaha

which is the mantram of the Green Tara

&, it seems, of all the other Taras, too
(who is Samaya-Tara & how does she relate to the Green Tara?)
& the occasion of this autobiographical interlude in the light poem in memoriam
Gustav Mahler
is my recent memory of my earliest encounter with the Green Tara
somewhere around my 8th year if not earlier
it was a movie starring the British actor
George Arliss
He's the sinister high priest of this Tibetan mountain
temple or monastery or something dedicated to "THE GREEN GODDESS"
which was the film's title
there are still probably prints of this film around somewhere
I dont remember much
of the action of that film but it had to do with some westerners coming into this
place & getting stuck there probably prisoners of George Arliss the high priest of
(who else?)
the green goddess
(How did the person who wrote this flim
encounter the Green Tara?
By seeing a thanka of her?
by reading?
or by having witnessed somewhere an initiation or other ceremony?
How sinister they made Your Sadhana o Sister
o Mother of Boddhisattvas
whose power in us is the compassion that makes us ride the whirpool of sorrow
neither engulfed nor lightly floating away
om tare tuttare ture swaha
om tare tuttare ture swaha
om tare tuttare ture swaha
om tare touttaré touré souahhah
AUM TARÉ TOUTTARÉ TOURÉ swaha om tare tuttare ture swaha om tare tuttare ture swaha)
I remember of this film this enormous lookdown from this Himalayan fastness
presided over by George Arliss on behalf of the Green Goddess
the first view of
that lookdown gave me vertigo, remembering it does, & later some guy fell down it
or did something that got him falling down it George Arliss had told them so I
think (he had of course this British accent probably with a cast of mixed American
& British accents)
I want to see that film again I'm sure it was a talkie
I remember Arliss talking British   but did anyone even in the background music

chant ok   i meant to write om & i wrote ok   Why do I suddenly abjure capitals?
I don't.
              But I have seldom if ever chanted in the middle of a light poem
("Lighten up, Iris!" urged John Smead. &, she says, she did. That's how she learned.)
              Kalu initiated me into the vision of the green goddess
         & last weekend   hearing & talking with Tarthang   aroused this memory
(not a trivial one   it has a deep resonance when I look & try to hear it
partly it was due to the halo of prestige surrounding this film starring a great
British actor & my father was from Great Britain & proud of Arliss & his fame &
that was the main reason we were at it, I think,   but
                                                        did anyone in it chant
om tare tuttare ture swaha om tare tuttare ture swaha om tare tuttare ture swaha
Tārā makes the bitter sorrow of parting from the body of my beloved
                                                             work for Dharma
work for me
              what do I mean by this pretentious language?
What do I mean by this glib verb: "work"?
Will the vision of Tara   Tara green & shining & offering her infinite compassion
     transmute this longing sorrow into a glory
                                   Oh Gustav, I am here at our new loft
on North Moore Street   in Bloho
                         Your symphonies' records are still in the Bronx
I'm typing at this end with M-M asleep at the other in his room
                                                   I started composing
your light poem, Gustav, on my old IBM electric but this part is being written on
my Colombian Olivetti Lettera Vente-Due
                         (it's got a ñ & Ñ & ¨ (ö) & ´ (é) & £ = & !)
That's the lightest one I have so I brought it down here it has a new ribbon

I didn't "intend" this poem to get out-of-hand this way. I intended a fairly
orderly if long-winded poem leading fairly often from one light name to another.
What I get it this. Not as badly or hotly typed as Rochle Rochelle's new Light
Poem, but still another, ego-tripping diary (or is this the way to make the ego
trip?)
     a kinda journal of the (mind?)
                                   well the whatever experience was going on
while he sat in his new kitchen typing this section of his (whose? Oh, Gus's!)
new Light Poem.
              It looks like it's going to be a book.   Well, why not?
But look at it this way: 9 typescript pages devoted to the "G" of "Gustav"
& the Green Light that flows from that "G" as it shines, from the heart of the

Boddhisattva

        Amoghasiddhi

                Lord of the Circle

    Who with All Powers Accomplishes All Actions

                          & this Green Light

will not give way   to the Ultraviolet Light of "Gustav"'s "U"

The green light that says, "Go!"   The Green Light of Action-Accomplishing

           Wisdom

That wdve been the place to end it all (I mean this Light Oh this Light Poem)
& anyone but me or Mahler or Maw Stein or Ted Enslin or Bruckner or Ezra
maybe wdve ended the poem right there at the bottom of page 9, with "wisdom," or
rather, "Wisdom", right there centered at the bottom of the page. Wow, whatta way to
end a poem: "The Green Light of Action-Accomplishing
            Wisdom"
What phoney baloney. What do I know about "Action-Accomplishing Wisdom" or any other
kinda "Wisdom" or even just wisdom?   What do *I* know about that Green Light?
    Am I worshipping George Arliss's Green Goddess when I chant om tare tuttare ture
swaha?
      OM AH HUM VAJRA GURU PADMA SIDDHI HUM
                            AUM MANI PADME HUM
        OM TARE TUTTARE TURE SWAHA

                    What did Tarthang mean, what did you mean, Tarthang,
when you said that the Guru mantram   om ah hum vajra guru padma siddhi hum
  was more "powerful" than the others?
                        (That's my Climatrol gas furnance humming
& whistling as it warms up half the outdoors thru the holes in the hatch
where the skylight will be
                If intense envy, of whom? I will now be envious intensely.

Now that she will no longer sleep with me, I will be intensely envious of those who do.

282

"... compassion is exhilarated by negative situations."

                        comments Trungpa Rinpoche
speaking of the Fourth Day in the Bardo wherein Amitābha

                       the Buddha of Boundless
Light
the purified element of fire   "The red

           light
            of the skandha of perception

                    in its
basic

          puri-
    ty,

50th Light Poem: For Sharon—23 September 1975

Sunlight or hallway light,
no use to say I love you.

I'm on my way to the reading.
The subway noise is loud.

Ardent light or reticent light,
no use to say I love you

I wish I hadn't lost–misplaced
your birthday-present ear plugs.

Ordinary light, natural light:
no use to say I love you.

Thanks for all those presents.
Thanks for being my girl.

                                        1st night of autumn
                                        on the way to my
                                        CBGB reading

51ˢᵗ Light Poem: For Sharon Belle Mattlin, from her "Vocabulary"—begun 18 December 1975, finished 20 December

See a lemon laser emanate harmonies
as a shaman in Athens   no hellenist or hellion   hints at more
More than the star that lit satin as it shone in the north?
More than a stellar ballet o'er a tremolant stream?
More than Mars?

Let it be Sol   Let his beams shine on this mean isle
Let them be sent to treat or beat its ills
Let them be sent in time   Let them shine on it   Let's breathe
Let a tribal satori arise   Let a smile be

Let elation roil the hell slime
Let mirth liberate the horse in the brain's ashen stable
Let one be on one's mettle

Sham trembles at banter meant to shatter its shit
The heart remains to be seen

Then   neither brash nor in thrall   it'll seem as it is

None'll sneer at its sheen   None'll rail at it or shame it
No mob'll roll oe'r it   No mitt'll hit it   No blast'll shatter or tear it

Is it a throne or is it on a throne?   It is no other than its throne
It is to metal as a bell is
It is to earth as a tree   to a tree as the earth is

I tremble to tell the tale o' the heart's health
To embellish it is to stab it   To thrill at it is triteness
O beam o' the real   blest be the real   blest be the heart o' the heart
More than that I tell all I see   let me see all I tell

I see the heart shine in the breast as a star near morn
Its beams melt shame   No harm or ill remains
Tho the heart be a letter in braille to those that see not
it *is* a letter in braille to those that see not   Blest be the heart
Let's see it   The lion   The breath

52nd Light Poem: For Susan Quasha on her 26th birthday—9 January 1976

An hour before your surprise birthday party
I sit at my desk in the loft two blocks away from the loft where your party will be
with the light shining from two clamp reflector lights & another one
one that's a kind of student lamp I've screwed to a rectangular board
shining on my typewriter & on the random-digit book
the RAND one I've used for 16 years or so & that I used just now
to draw some light names from my old chart
using the letters in your name that are on the chart & random-digit couplets under 21
I don't know yet where I'll get the kinds of light for the other letters
for the 2 U's & the Q & the H
It's surprising how few other letters you have: how few different ones

I just had to leave a big white vertical space on the page
because as Baraka wrote when he was still Jones "Jackson Mac Low can't type."
I'm trying to write this before your party without mistakes on the page
but my correction fluid takes too long to dry
Does this throw an unusual light on my poetry?
I think Cage said he retained question marks because they are touching

Two of the reflector lights are shining into my eyes
but the light from the goosenecked smaller reflector light that's like a student lamp
is shaded from my eyes
They're all shaded lights but the reflecting shades don't help with two of them
the one to my right that's shining on the random-digit book
& the one to the left clamped to the crosspiece of the window
I'm not going to try to avoid mistakes any more
It's 8:55 & I'll x them out from now on
I guess this poem's about the experience of writing this poem in this way
& I guess it's for you on your birthday because this experience wdntve taken place
if I wasnt about to go to your surprise birthday party
& I hadnt not had time to buy you a present somewhere

Mordecai was just hyperventilating & I asked him why
he said to knock himself out or get near doing that

There are 3 children in the loft right now, as well as Sharon & me

Mordecai-Mark, Clarinda, & Sharon's young half-sister, Jessica
Look how I'm using commas now I began using commas at 9 PM
I wonder how I can make the shift to the Aurora Borealis

Yes I have to shift to talking about the Aurora Borealis
I saw it in Woodstock or rather in Bearsville in the Fall of 1946
& I saw it on Cape Breton Island
the summer of 1971
That was the summer after Iris left & when we had that poetry festival in Michigan
You & George were there & a lot of our other friends
Paul Blackburn was still alive I guess that reading was the last he gave
Armand & the Rothenbergs & the Kellys were there
Right after it I had to go into the French Hospital
I'd discovered not long before that I had a double inguinal hernia
2 hernias at the groin one on each side at least theyre symmetrical
So after the poetry festival I had Dr. Newman sew them up
That's why I have stainless-steel sutures in me beneath my pubic hair
& my friend Bici who'd come out a month or so before
saw me into the hospital & visited me every day
& after I got out & I was convalescing in her house
we became better friends than we'd been for the five or so years before
Her husband had taken their two kids & mine up to their place on Cape Breton Island
& as soon as I was well enough the two of us flew up there
& lived together in a tent for the month of August
One night after we'd been making love in the tent
voices called us & lights shined on the tent
& everyone was running to the top of the hill to see the Aurora Borealis
It was shining & theater-curtaining over the Gulf of St. Lawrence
It was cold already up there & we first sat watching it outside wrapped in a blanket
Later I think we went to the hill but maybe we didnt
That was the 2nd of only 2 times I saw the Aurora Borealis

& now theyre trying to outlaw Napalm flames in warfare
a Queer kind of light to bring in now after the Aurora Borealis?
An unprepared light? I havent prepared this jump at all
This is the way it goes when one sits writing about seeing the Aurora Borealis
in the light from a kind of student lamp but really a goodenecked reflector lamp
mounted on a small raw rectangular board
Well both napalm & the northern lights might be called heavenly light
they come down from the heavens or stay up there better they stay up there
Who can imagine napalm flames dropping on people

people burning with jellied gasoline all over them
till nothing's left of the people except a kind maybe of afterglow
This is nothing to think about on the occasion of a birthday
except for some Buddhists & such who always think of birth & death & rebirth together

Is that genuine do any of us really think about rebirth when we really think about
living & dying & pleasuring & paining & all the things we do & that happen to us
from the Aurora Borealis to the Napalm Flames
What do we do when we think about being born & about the day when we were born
coming again that date coming again on the calendar & then we celebrate it
& our friends & our parents & children & all all wish us happy birthday
& they give us nice things presents not napalm flames but not aurora borealises either
altho the last time I saw the aurora borealis was pretty near my own birthday that year
That was the year I turned 49 the last birthday I had I turned 53
Right now it's 9:26 & I'm nearly 53 & 1/3 years old
& I truly cant remember if I ever knew how old you are
so I left a blank space in the title to fill it in later to tell which birthday
I'm writing this light poem for you at my desk in the loft 2 blocks
away from the surprise birthday party that's supposed to happen in about 2 minutes

Sharon says "It's almost 9:30." & that's why I'm going to stop writing this now
May light shine on you & from you for years & years & years

53rd Light Poem: For Stephanie Vevers—12–13 December 1976–21 & 28
February 1978

What spectrum of twinkling lights for Stephanie?

My exit light's burnt out. Shall I replace it?
That plastic-shielded bulb cast a hellish glow. I liked it.
That artificial light lied "EXIT" on its 'scutcheon:
thru the door *this* way's more of a way out than into the cold!
Coming in from the cold just now & all that tense craziness:
Bruce Ditmas at The Kitchen exploding into yellow healing violence
on drums & cymbals & synthesizers:
sitting in the front row was like what being fistfucked must be like
& maybe more dangerous to the ears than that to the bowels.
Tom Johnson & others sat with fingers in ears or hands over them
but I welcomed that violence like the naked light of an incendiary bomb.
Like like like what are all these similes doing here?
That violent young man with long hair & beard, dark & piratical,
whose tee shirt shouted "WIZARD RECORDS," & whose partner, Joan La Barbara,
bright, slender composer-performer with voice & electrons, Bruce's girl friend,
carefully videotaped that violent concert:
that's the second time I tried to type out "girl friend"—*that* was the third:
each time I've first typed the "i" as if typing "fire."

Into this pleasant loft kitchen, an exit from all that tense craziness:
looking across my plants I see the ITT Building's night lights
(I thought that art-deco classic was ITT's when I first wrote this,
but by the time I learned it was Western Union's,
ITT was in the poem for good):
lights of ITT, producers of torturers & their field telephones
—it is called the "parrot's beak"—that position they tie people into
when they shove one electrode up their ass & the other up their—
I can't seem to type "urethra"—or up their vagina?
The Becks labeled their field telephone mock-up "ITT"
when they did their piece on political sadomasochism,
& they had a guy tied up over a bar that way—very pornographic:
Paul Goodman wd've called it sadopornographic,
& he'd've been right—as so often he was.
All that tense craziness: not Bruce or even the ITT— as if typing "fire"—
the famous fires of jealousy & ludicrously inflated desire

(I learned to use "famous" that way from Paul)
—just last night & today I think I've learned to damp those fires—fancy it up:
"purge those purgatorial fires" from my relation with Sharon:
I don't have to desire her any more.

[Note: There are two extant typescripts of this poem. The first, dated December 12–13, 1976, was subject to corrections by hand on several occasions over the next fourteen months, up until February 21, 1978. On retyping the poem one week later, JML concluded at this point. It is unclear whether or not he intended to include the following text. —Eds.]

I don't have to feel jealous of another.
(We met John near her place as we walked to her door,
a sweet philosophy-studying man with long blond hair & beard.)

What a pleasure to have dinner in Chinatown with my children & Sharon,
attend Bruce's concert with her, walk her home, meet John & his brother,
leave her safely at her door, press her hand goodbye, & walk back here,
feeling only attenuated twinges of desire & jealousy:
I sincerely smiled sweetly at John, hoping to reassure him:
as long as they see each other once in a while,
I think I don't have to desire her anymore:
we can be finally friends after all this tense craziness:
I love her dearly but now without the tense craziness: it's over.
We can play music without the tense craziness jangling the overtones.
(That's a lie: we never jangled the overtones: the show went on:
never "Ridi, Pagliacci!" even—we give ourselves to the tones:
the tones launch out from us: we're the Muses' machines: watch us vibrate!)

What a crazy light poem to write for Stephanie Vevers!
She shows me things, she gives me the world, she makes me see what I forgot to look at any-
more (this is the first line that's gone past the right margin!).
Not so crazy:
remember that card I sent you from Milwaukee airport a month ago, the one with the quote
from Emerson about a how a friend was someone you cd think out loud in front of?
You said you weren't at all sure you wanted to think out loud in front of *any*one: no, can't in
your talk, at all!
But I have that old-fashioned self-revealing need.
(Self-revealing? I'm probably lying through my teeth!)
I think I have the need to let you see me:
Please like me enough to indulge my exhibitionism!

Oh honesty! Honesty! What a pile of shit that word is!

I'm sitting at my Colombian Olivetti 22
with the "ñ" and the accent & the umlaut & the pound sign
(I guess that umlaut's a dieresis):
I seem to be making a profession of being vulnerable in poems like this:
I seem to be telling the truth & I'm probably lying thru my teeth.

Thru my teeth.

What an enigmatic light is thrown on a poet's life by his words!
Maybe if I didn't try to be honest things'd come out better & realer!

Why have I come to value you so highly?
Not just the swirling milky patterns on the river's surface,
not just the scaling paint on the old police car-pound we walked out beside
(the walk beside it gave us the river's dragons).
I know I'm oversimplifying you when I say you look at things with clear eyes:
not an innocent eye, a knowing one: a woman in a girl's body.

The "light of the void": mere Buddhist cant or ultimate truth?

I sit in a little chair at the yellow vinyl table top perched on 2 little barrels:
the long kitchen table you've sometimes eaten with us at,
the one we sat at & played with the Lite-Brite on for hours
after the rehearsal Christopher Knowles rushed away from
to go to the balcony & play with two of them, laughing with joy
(one of Chris's Lite-Brites had only blue pegs in it, like that kind of Xmas tree),

where we sat listening to the tapes of the Bessie Smith memorial
our benefit in a bar for WIN, the pacifist magazine—
beautiful live musicians & records,
but hardly any audience;
where we listened to tapes of Meredith's Town Hall Concert & part of Phil Glass's Einstein—
the last time you were here we stayed up nearly till dawn copying that
(alas! my JVC mini cassette recorder now puts motorboat sounds on everything:
it's served me well since I bought it at the Keflavik duty-free store
just a year & a half ago on my way back from England:
now it puts motorboat sounds on everything).
All of those simple moments the vivid light of the void burst out of for me
(I don't pretend anything like that happened for you,
just as I don't pretend just hanging around with me makes you as happy
as just hanging around with you makes me)

I dont think I'm talking about love or desire.
Maybe I'm afraid of the banalities of love & desire.
I know I love to share looking & hearing with you
& embraces of antediluvian chasteness.
I know you arent the only person
who can shed an enchanting light on the emerging occasions as they happen me,
as I happen the emerging occasions.
That's pretty stuff: "enchanting light"—makes everything seem so happy:
I expect the light of the void's a lot more violent:
outrageous Trungpa'd opt for all that tense craziness:
"Feel the lust. Feel the jealousy. Transmute them into wisdoms.
Swig the poisons down and make them nectar!"

People talk about "hurting" & "not hurting":
You don't do such-&-such so's not to hurt So-&-So:
your mother & your aunt talk a lot that way
—persons of such good will it breaks my heart to realize
how time has twisted their lifelines, tamed their hearts!—
& my heart sinks when you too talk about "hurting":
better Bruce's electric-arc-light violence
whapping those drums & cymbals & Moog transducers & breaking drumsticks
(but then I remember that other kind of violence:
Robin's and crazy Bill Kehoe's
—not healing vivid yellow like Bruce's drumbeats,
that after-all-orderly violence let out upon consenting bodies in our neighborhood
        performance loft—

but the real violence, the real void, unmitigated by art)
& even tho I've seen lives withered by such violence as theirs,
what is theirs compared to the Shah's & the Junta's torturers'?
(Different lights are on in the ITT Building now than when I first looked.
Different torturers are cranking field telephones burning different victims.)

No that's cheap rhetoric like that of the cheapjack "revolutionaries"—
give the audience a cheap thrill by mentioning torture!

Better the violence of lust & love!
Better the orderly violence of sadomasochistic rituals between consenting bodies,
consenting spirits,
better Bruce whapping his drums & cymbals, fistfucking our eardrums!

Better than what?

Than the violence that withers lives bit by bit by not hurting, I mean, hurting by trying
          not to hurt,
or the violence that withers lives by callous & even knowing hurting,
or the violence that suddenly blasts lives apart for reasons of state,
or the violence . . .

It's strange how much I've come to speak of violence in your light poem:
your clear unsentimental gentleness engenders thoughts of its opposite.

Superlatives! Superlatives!
I keep thinking: "You cast such a reasonable light, such scintillating light, on everything
          we talk about!"

That seems to *have* to get into the poem even tho it sounds like silly compliments.
You of all people don't need silly compliments & it's not silly compliments.
I'm sitting here at twenty to four in the morning with my gas furnace whistling & roaring
          & my Olivetti snapping & crackling,
& as they used to say, "God save the mark!"—I'm trying to tell the truth as it comes along.

It's a priggish thing to keep trying to tell the truth & all that—
maybe better to make pretty & forget about truth
(sometimes pretty's truer than selfconscious ugly "truth")
I'm thinking of the really pretty performances we did of my music in Buffalo last Sunday:
that strange ensemble, two trombones, flute, guitar, & celeste, & all our voices:
pretty was very true—very few false notes—

I've heard the tape often enough to be sure of it [I want you to hear it]:
all that mostly quiet sensitive sound was true to the emerging occasions.)

In & out of parentheses, the poem wanders as it pleases,
even tho the light names spelling your name pretend to armature it.

I don't remember the quote from Emerson
on that corny card I sent you from Milwaukee airport,
so I look up his essay on friendship:

"We have a great deal more kindness than is ever spoken. Maugre all the self-
ishness that chills like east winds the world, the whole human family is bathed with an
element of love like a fine ether. How many persons we meet in houses, whom we scarcely
speak to, whom yet we honor, and who honor us! How many we see in the street, or sit
with in church, whom, though silently, we warmly rejoice to be with! Read the language
of these wandering eye-beams. The heart knoweth."

& later on:

"High thanks I owe you, excellent lovers, who carry out the world for me to new
and noble depths, and enlarge the meaning of all my thoughts."

&:

"I ought to be equal to every relation."

"I do not wish to treat friendships daintily, but with roughest courage. When
they are real, they are not glass threads or frostwork, but the solidest thing we know."

& here it is:

"A friend is a person with whom I may be sincere. Before him I may think aloud.
I am arrived at last in the presence of a man so real and equal, that I may drop even
those undermost garments of dissimulation, courtesy, and second thought, which men
never put off, and may deal with him with the simplicity and wholeness with which one
chemical atom meets another. Sincerity is the luxury allowed, like diadems and authority,
only to the highest rank, *that* being permitted to speak truth, as having none above it to
court or conform unto. Every man alone is sincere. [That I doubt, dear Ralph: if only it
were true!] At the entrance of a second person, hypocrisy begins. We parry and fend the
approach of our fellow-man by compliments, by gossip, by amusements, by affairs. We
cover up our thought from him under a hundred folds. [We cover up our thoughts from

ourselves, Ralph, under a hundred folds!] I knew a man, who, under a certain religious frenzy, cast off this drapery, and, omitting all compliment and commonplace, spoke to the conscience of every person he encountered, and that with great insight and beauty. At first he was resisted, and all men agreed he was mad. But persisting, as indeed he could not help doing, for some time in this course, he attained to the advantage of bringing every man of his acquaintance into true relations with him. No man would think of speaking falsely with him, or of putting him off with any chat of markets or reading-rooms. But every man was constrained by so much sincerity to the like plaindealing, and what love of nature, what poetry, what symbol of truth he had, he did certainly show him. But to most of us, society shows not its face and eye, but its side and its back. To stand in true relations with men in a false age is worth a fit of insanity, is it not? We can seldom go erect. Almost every man we meet requires some civility, —requires to be humored; he has some fame, some talent, some whim of religion or philanthropy in his head that is not to be questioned, and which spoils all conversation with him. But a friend is a sane man who exercises not my ingenuity, but me. My friend gives me entertainment without requiring any stipulation on my part. A friend, therefore, is a sort of paradox in nature. I who alone am, I who see nothing in nature whose existence I can affirm with equal evidence to my own, behold now the semblance of my being, in all its height, variety, and curiosity, reiter-ated in a foreign form; so that a friend may well be reckoned the masterpiece of nature.

"The other element of friendship is tenderness."

How I love your reasonable, gentle voice, Ralph!

I forgive all the horrors of sadistic truthtelling, encounter groups, stabbing frankness, that sprang from these gentle, reasonable, reasonable words of yours & your comrades, Ralph (you with your "man" & "he" & "him" & "fellow-man" —
didn't Margaret have something to say about *that*, Ralph?)—I forgive—*almost* forgive—
the legacy of boorishness & callousness that misunderstanding of such words let to—
when I hear your gentle, reasonable, tender voice.

"The other element of friendship is tenderness."

"I wish that friendship should have feet, as well as eyes and eloquence. It must plant itself on the ground, before it vaults over the moon."

I cd quote you, Ralph, all day, but whose poem wd it be then?
"We chide the citizen because he makes love a commodity."
I have to shut the book on all that beautiful talk.
I want to talk to you, dear live Stephanie, not you, dear dead Ralph!
Not true, I want to talk to both of you. I love you both so dearly!

I wish I cd talk to your spirit, Ralph, as I can talk to you, Stephanie, now.
(Dear Marilyn in Chicago has often spoken to her spirit friends:
she introduced me once to one who said I looked like a saint & if not a saint, a buffalo hunter
—Libby Fideaux has a fine sense of humor—but do I quite believe in her?
I hope she's for real because I've loved Marilyn Fillis since we were in high school:
the only person beside my father I visited in Chicago on the way back from Milwaukee.)

I've never had the sense to know where "friendship" left off & "love" began:
Sharon says I want to sleep with everyone I like
hyperbole but nearly true, tho contrary to what's happening:
I seldom exchange or share sexual acts with anyone, even myself:
she mostly does with John, now: she & I seldom:
we may never do so again (I wonder what you really thought about sex, Ralph!)
but during the last few months
I've learned the wonderful joys of the chaste embrace,
of bodies tenderly held in each other's arms
(as Alkibiades said Sokrates held him)
with little desire or none beyond that tender holding:
an amazing depth of happiness has grown in me from that simple act:
my friend can hardly believe she's given & shared such pleasure
(not Ralph, but some of his Transcendental friends did this:
how long, before muddy Eros had his way,
before great Aphrodite filled their limbs with longing—
if Sokrates never sucked off Alkibiades,
did Alkibiades never try to do *him*?—
Did no one on Brook Farm keep a sexual journal?)

Wd Ralph have said today:
"I wish that friendship should have genitals, as well as eyes and eloquence"?

Silly dirty old man: haven't you learned yet to leave that to others?
To the young & those whose bodies bring them lovers?

Sitting at ten after six, typing at the kitchen table,
admitting the fire's still burning just beneath the skin,
tho part of me wants to put it out entirely,
hoping the joys of the chaste embrace'll endure and grow,
knowing I want to share —How the iron shutters are banging in the wind!
How the mylar over the holes in my roof flaps & slaps in the wind!
My Olivetti's quiet tapping's drowned in the iron sounds BANG BOOM!
The corny symbols are overwhelming this quietness.

The rain & the wind—I want I want I want:
"Lust & Rage, Lust & Rage," sang ancient Yeats.
My pleasure at being overwhelmed by Bruce's violence:
my stifling desire & coming back here to write all night:
BANG BONK BOOM!

Lust & Rage
Lust & Rage
Lust & Rage

54th Light Poem: For Ian Tyson—4:54 PM 27 June 1977

Description & Instructions

The "54th Light Poem: For Ian Tyson" combines features of several "genres" I've developed since 1961.   First, it is a "Light Poem," a "genre" first developed in June 1962 (see *22 Light Poems*, Los Angeles: Black Sparrow Press, 1968) & continued in various ways since then. All Light Poems mention light, or names of kinds of light, but in composing most of them, I have drawn light names, mostly by chance operations, from a chart of 288 such names prepared in June 1962.   In composing the "54th Light Poem," I drew from the chart, using chance operations, a series of light names whose initial letters successively spell out "Ian Tyson" (e.g., p. 1, 1. 6, "illucidation"; 1. 9, "aurora australis" & "napalm").   However, when I reached "y," I had to introduce a light name not on the chart (p. 3, 1. 3, "YaNg not Yankee lights), since none there begins with "y."

In addition, his name is spelled out "diastically" in the red capital letters: the lines are so written that the letters of his name slant down thru each two strophes, alternately of three lines ("IAN") & five lines ("TYSON"): "I" appears in the first square of line 1, "A" in the 2nd square of line 2, &c.   I began using "diastic" (having letters of index words, such as names, appear in corresponding places in lines) as against "acrostic" (index words' letters appearing initially or finally in lines) as a chance-selection method in January 1963, after having previously used acrostic extensively (e.g., in *Stanzas for Iris Lezak*, Barton, Vt.: Something Else Press, 1972; & subsequently in the 501 numbered "Asymmetries").   However, from 1963 until March 1977, when I wrote "Fifteen Quinzains for Stephanie Vevers" (see *Roof* VI, Spring 1978: 64–68, the first part of *Traditional Verse*, a collection of such series, the diastic was "hidden," merely serving to generate the poem. But in the Quinzains & similar series, the index words appear openly, as a line of capital letters in a contrasting color of typeface, slanting down thru each poem.   The "54th Light Poem" is the first of my poems not generated primarily by chance operations in which index words ("IAN TYSON") are placed diastically.

Finally, the poem is a "Gatha," a "genre" developed first in 1961. In previous Gathas, letters of mantras, & after 1973 of nonmantric words, are placed, primarily thru chance operations, on quadrille graph paper,

& the resulting configurations are used, as described below, as "scores" for performances in which performers make spontaneous choices. All Gathas composed thru 1978 will appear in *First Book of Gathas* (Milwaukee: Membrane Press, 1979).

INSTRUCTIONS: The poem may be performed by one or more readers. It is first read from beginning to end by one reader thoroughly familiar with the poem, who uses the words' placement on the grid & an understanding derived from careful reading to group the words into complete utterances, despite the lack of punctuation. Pauses, stresses, & other appropriate elocutionary devices must be used to bring out the meaning of this very personal poem.

Then it is performed *as a Gatha* by that reader & the others, if any: each reader starts at any square & "moves" to any square adjacent to its sides or corners. One may say *names* of letters, *sounds* of letters, *syllables* formed by letters adjacent in any direction, & *words, phrases* or other *word strings*, or *whole sentences*, either found in the poem itself or formed by grouping letters in nonhorizontal directions, as well as horizontally.

Once one has started reading *words of the poem*, one may continue by reading from succeeding lines. Thus, each reader may incorporate portions of the poem of various lengths in the "Gatha" section of the performance, as well as letter names & sounds, syllables, words &c.

In addition to following "paths" from square to square on single pages of the poem, performers must, every so often, "leap" from one part of a page to another, & from one page to another. They may freely go back & forth, from one part of the poem to another, throughout a performance.

Performers must *listen* intently to all sounds produced by other performers, by the audience, or in the environment, & must *modify* their performances accordingly. "Listen!" & "Relate!" are the most important "rules." One may *repeat* sounds, syllables, words, word groups, & so on; make "*loops*," i.e., repeatedly follow a path among the squares that crosses itself; or *prolong* vowels, semivowels, laterals, nasal, sibilants, or fricatives. If one person begins to prolong a sound, others may wish also to prolong sounds, producing prolonged intervals or chords which may act as "organ points" under the play of shorter sounds.

Empty squares must always be interpreted as *silences* of any duration. These silences ought often be *prolonged* until one feels one can add positively to the total situation. Since everything depends upon the performers' choices made spontaneously during performances, awareness, sensitivity, tact, courtesy, & inspiration must be one's guides, & one must often *listen silently* for quite a while before adding anything new to the situation.

A performance may be open-ended or have its duration set before it begins. The former may be ended by spontaneous consensus of performers or by one chosen as leader who gives an ending signal when it is felt appropriate. The latter may be ended by a leader or by a device that gives an inaudible signal, such as a flashing light.

54th Light Poem for Ian Tyson
4:54 pm 27 June 1977

I'm going to tell a light story
SAying something on this grid
CoNcerning my friend who loves
                            grids

Sing The fascination of the grid
FlightY Muse of Light Poetry
What muSe else will rise to sing
Grids' lOvers & their loves
Is there No muse of networks

Illucidation of quadrille paper
PAper that's quadrillé by rules
LiNes intersecting at right
        angles & equal intervals
                forming squares

Oh AusTralis Oh Aurora Oh Napalm
TertiarY qualities separate you
QualitieS irrelevant to light
On John LOcke's metaphysical map
Oh GridiroN whereon we yet roast

I wdnt be surprised to find that
IAn Tyson thinks I'm lunatescent
DoNt forget you read it here 1st

FirsT sing Ian's meticulous hand
LoudlY across these thirty-two
GoddesS Sappho called Netweaver
You O DOLOPLOKA APHRODITA sing
Ian QueeN Muse of Gridirons sing

301

```
PAGE  2   54TH   LIGHT  POEM  29  June
          FOR  IAN  TYSON  12:30  AM   7 7

Ian    near   Thameside    Tower    Bridge
PAttterning    his    left    shoulder    sky
SuN    in    his    eyes    makes    him    frown

In    sTrain    is    how    I    see    Ian    Tyson
AworrYing    in    his    river    warehouse
What    iS    Ian    Tyson    worrying    about
Break    loose    Ian    smudge    the    grids
No    screeN    of    lines    between

Ian    you    &    the    colors'    chaos    &    us
BArs    evoke    jails    in    any    contexts
FaNtasies    of    Ian's    wrath    arise
               How    many    times    has    he
               been    subjected    to
               this    vulgar
          psychoanalitic    reproach

What    is    This    bullshit    about    bars
So    say    whY    you    compartmentalize
What's    looSening    your    lines    Ian
Ach    youve    lOst    half    the    gridiron
O    InstitutioNs    fall    as    easily

If    I    dont    pry    into    your    life    how
IAn    can    I    throw    any    light    on    you
NoNe    asked    you    to    throw    anything

LighT    or    darkness    or    rice    grains
LovelY    colors    sable    squares    hold
NonsenSe    Only    relationsre    lovely
Never    cOlors    per    se    hardly    ever
Ian    TysoN    in    tertiary    radiation
```

302

```
54TH   LIGHT   POEM   1   JULY   77
       FOR   IAN   TYSON        11 : 21   PM

Is   either   lethal   or   dangerous   or
TAme   as   banal   diagnostic   X   rays
YaNg   not   Yankee   lights   for   Ian   T.

Ian   Tyson   sits   in   shadowed   light
RichlY   pied   by   orgone   lumination
No   boiSterous   noonday   light   here
It   is   now   3 : 20   AM   Thu   15   Sept   77
It's   eveNing   now   8 : 14   PM   9 / 15 / 77

It   is   now   11   PM   Fri   16   Sept   1977
MAhler's   5th   plays   on   the   stereo
CaN   I   turning   see   her   I   love   yes

Now   Theatrical   lights   may   dazzle
BeautY's   yeasaying   light   dazzles
Truth'S   smoking   lamp's   kymograph
Can   recOrd   only   on   this   darkness
FalsifyiNg   hearts   radiate   calmly

In   this   darkness   we   move   breathe
EAt   think   perceive   love   grow   die
CaN   we   make   our   mark   on   any   else

TrusT   no   light   from   oil   gas   here
DarklY   understand   brightly   know
DarkneSs   slate   for   truth's   chalk
Dark   grOund   needlelined   by   truth
IllumiiNg   thru   &   by   means   of   it

I   end   Ian's   grid   light   poem   song
TAlking   epistemology's   mysteries
WaNTrappings   of   dumb   Illuminati
TwentY   times   better   confessional
IE   gossSipy   poetry   than   idealized
GuttatiOn   of   verbal   debris   as   is
Shine   a   Naked   light   on   Ian   Tyson
```

55th Light Poem: Unwritten

[No evidence of a 55th Light Poem has been discovered. Note that at the outset of the 56th Light Poem, Mac Low questions his numbering of the poem. —Eds.]

56th Light Poem: For Gretchen Berger—29 November 1978

From Gretchen's "G" I get a green light. I go ahead.
The first Light Poem in nearly a year—I hope it really *is* the
        56th.
If there's another in some notebook or file folder,
it's the one that's going to get its number changed, not this
        one
This is the 56th Light Poem, & I'm 56 years old.
I *was* 56 September 12th. Time has passed. I'm older now.

I sit at the back of the loft, typing on a little low table,
since it's too cold to type at my desk by the middle west window
        whose cracks I stuffed with Mortite caulking yesterday.
It'll be warmer, I hope, after Mordecai covers that window with
        plastic.
Until then I'll type out here, surrounded by papers, dictionaries,
file folders, notebooks, Coronamatic cartridges.
Is this the word "Coronamatic"'s first appearance in verse?

Would Eliot've allowed "Coronamatic" in his verse?
If so, under what circumstances?
Would he only have written it ironically or satirically?
Can you imagine "Coronamatic"
in one of the *Four Quartets*?
Can you guess how Eliot crept into this Light Poem at this point?

Relucence of the *Four Quartets* illuminates this verse
because I reread most of the group the other day.
A reviewer of Helen Gardner's new book on them mentions a line
dropped from the New York edition—probably through printer's
        error—
that Gardner's recovered—which shows some critics are useful.
It's the real 20th line of "Little Gidding."

He begins: "Midwinter spring is its own season
Sempiternal though sodden towards sundown,/Suspended in time,...
... the hedgerow/Is blanched for an hour with transitory blossom
Of snow, a bloom more sudden
Than that of summer, neither budding nor fading,
Not in the scheme of generation."

Then that first strophe ends with *three* lines, not two.
Where was the middle line lost—here or in London or between?
Did someone who thought it useless drop it on purpose?
"Where is the summer, the unimaginable
Summer beyond sense, the inapprehensible
Zero summer?"

Could Eliot have dropped that line on purpose
while he was correcting the New York proofs?
A major shift in meaning occurs from "the unimaginable
Summer beyond sense, the inapprehensible/Zero summer"
to "the unimaginable/Zero summer":
the words left out imply another view of the nature of things.

As if electric-arc light had replaced
"The brief sun" that "flames the ice, on ponds and ditches,…
Reflecting in a watery mirror
A glare that is blindness in the early afternoon"—
or tungsten light, the "glow more intense than blaze of branch, or brazier,"
that "Stirs the dumb spirit: no wind, but pentecostal fire"!

Why do I care so much that Eliot's line was left out
when a chart & two random digits lead to the light of a clutch lamp
"(an arc-lamp in which the upper carbon
is adjusted automatically by a clutch)"—
fortuitously connecting with the "electric-arc light" above,
though there could've been an absolute disconnection?

How much of the halcyon light of the poet's mind
was lost when someone working in electric-lamp light
forgot to set that line—& no one caught it?
Why do words implying an alien philosophy
move me more than—I was going to say "nova light":—
but how do I know how I'd feel if I saw a real nova–not just a photo?

The light of poetry's a baffling light.
It doesn't depend on what the poet thinks—or even what he feels!
That extra light that gave old Housman goose bumps
comes from somewhere beyond or underneath
thought or emotion or will or taste or sense:
a radiation only known through words.

That glow can be snuffed out
by burning a book or slitting a throat
or sleepily nodding in a stuffy composing room,
but coming from somewhere more arcane
than an exploding star whose light spans light-years,
it momently arcs a rainbow through existence.

57th Light Poem: For John Taggart—on & about & after the Ides, March 1979

A jewel-like light gleams at the end of a passage,
an orange light hazy through distance,
diffused through innumerable layers of air:
to those in hiding a horrible light,
to the children who hide in a house from the roaring
& the leaping light of flaming napalm,
to those who love the children who hide in a house from the roaring,
that tiny light no brighter than that of an alchohol lamp
but lacking all blueness,
that light glimmering forward down the hallway
toward the children
& those who love the children,
hiding in perfect stillness,
that light might as well
be burning incinder jell.

What if it were the glorious light
in which they might delight
to lift up their heads without effort to sing,
in which the children who hide in the house from the roaring
& the leaping light of flaming napalm
& those who love the children
might
delight
in lifting up their heads without effort to sing as a chorus,
the men & women holding hands with the children to go
forward as a chorus without burden?

What if that gemlike light were harbinger
of dancing & singing unburdened as the morning stars
amid the permutations of the bells?

Silent as curtains of aurora borealis
billowing high across northern skies
suffused with a shifting rose light,
an eerily transcendental light,
the jewel light approaches the children & women & men from the end
   of the shadowy passage.

Is it the light of an olive-oil lamp?
It is the only light in the hall,
unechoed by mirrors,
revealing no form.

To the children & women & men who love each other
hiding in perfect stillness at the hall's end
a pitiless noonlight approaches.

The night wind blows.

No form is revealed in the hall's growing twilight
to those standing hand in hand in hiding,
that loving chorus silent as an aurora.

In the gray light growing through the hallway air
no hands are revealed, no elbows & no face,
no torso & no legs; no feet are seen.

That gemlike light approaches in a dream of terror
those in hiding know they'll never awake from.

It blinds them like an arc light.

What is the good of standing hand in hand in perfect stillness
as radiance crushes forth toward their trapped light?

58th Light Poem: For Anne Tardos—19–20 March 1979

I

I know when I've fallen in love   I start to write love songs
Love's actinism turns nineteens to words & thoughts in love songs
as your "A" & the date made "actinism" enter this love song

Also I seem to start dropping punctuation
My need for punctuation lessens   like some people's need for sleep
My need for sleep lessens too   but later I fall on my face
Lack of punctuation doesn't catch up with me like lack of sleep
It doesn't make me fall on my face

So bright the near noon light   the toy photometer twirls   in
the sunlight slanting in from southeast thru the southwest window
the stronger the light the faster the light motor turns
diamond vanes' black sides absorb   white sides radiate photons
See it go

A "42" draws the northern lights into the song
as yesterday into the Taggart Light Poem twice they were drawn
as "aurora borealis" & "aurora" by "A" 's & by numbers
There they seemed eery & threatening   Here they seem hopeful
as they seemed when last I saw them over the Gulf of St. Lawrence
cold   euphoric after making love   wondering
at swirling curtains & sudden billows lighting the sky northwest

I remember their evanescent light as neutral or bluish white
I remember the possibility of yellow   the improbability of red
not like Bearsville's rose & blood sky twenty-five years before
Now these memories mingled with pictures' descriptions'
project on inward skies   idiosyncratic northern lights
that only exist while I'm writing these lines for Anne
Even the next time I read them the lights they arouse will be different

Nineteen sheds a tranquil light on our love song thru your "T"
Our love's tranquil light   revelaed by 19 & by T
is turned by 15 to an aureole tipping an "A"
The "A" becomes your face   The aureole grows

Relucence from my face glows back on yours

A telephone bell can deflect & dissipate my light
The deflected light is lost to poem & person
I turn my telephone off these days to help ordinary light breed poems

The sun is so bright on my desk now   except on the typewriter keys
that there's no need for the light of the student lamp placed to shine
    on the paper

But now   five hours later   the lamp's   the only light
& I begin the poem's   "astrological"   section

II

Acetylene light may be what Virgo needs to see the "pattern
except that for him this is something" he will
only acknowledge if it can be seen in natural light

Can we gain new light from astrology   that ubiquitous superstition
You Sagittarius Woman   Me Virgo Man
What "can happen between them is a" mazing
a dizzying   a stupefying or dazing   a crazing
a great perplexing   bewildering   amazing
forming a maze of something or making it intricate

being bewildered   wandering as is a maze
What has happened between them is amazing

What is happening between us is amazing
more intense & vivid than electric arc light   tremendous light
brighter than acetylene light   friendly as reading lamp light

"But a young Sagit-
tarian need have no qualms about taking on a
man considerably her senior if he is a Virgo"
Rand's random digits underline our case
in this lovely silly optimistic sentence

We've been living I think in a kind of drowning light

"He reaches the age of forty   At anything less than that age
he is not even a possible   for Sagittarius"
Me Virgo Man   You Sagittarius Woman
Orgone radiation flimmers between us
our curious safety light

"What can happen between them is   superb
Something he has spent half his life dreaming about
At last it has come true"   O ingratiating
astrological light may you never prove false
even to one who has often decried you as no light
but superstitious darkness natural light would dispel
or the electric arc light of empirical science

The way I'm writing this poem's like using
trichromatic artificial radiance
not as decorative light   in place of
ordinary solar radiation   as you photographers do

Before I was forty "not even a possible for Sagittarius"
now I'm sixteen over the line & safe with you

"Her   but a young Sagittarian need have" none   "qualms" have no
  basis

Are we dreaming   Is this Virgo man still dreaming
as "he has spent half his life"   they say   "dreaming"

"Sagittarian & Virgo"
"The pattern is perfect"
The poem is over

59th Light Poem: For La Monte Young and Marian Zazeela—6 November 1982

Late light allows us to begin.
Altair's light on an altar guides us onward.

Many lights are seen where mountains cluster.
Orange lights are spangled over hillsides.
Neutral light glows above their ridges.
Tiny lights of many kinds begin to be discernible.
Evanescent lights arise and die.

Yellow light momently overspreads.
Ochre light succeeds it.
Umber light in a while is all that is left.
Nearly nonexistent light increases rapidly.
Green light envelops everything.

Magenta light glows over the farther peaks.
Alabaster lights suddenly shoot upward.
Red lights cross the sky diagonally.
Incandescent-lamp light glows in the foreground.
Acetylene-lamp light splits the ambience.
No light at all supervenes.

Zodiacal light replaces light's absence.
Algae-green light maculates the glow.
Zincz light flares amid the highest oaks.
Escaping light illumes Lithuanian paths.
Earthlight grows near the Baltic.
Lithuanian light lessens environing earthlight.
All the light there *can* be won't be enough.

60th Light Poem: *In Memoriam* Robert Duncan—8–9 October 1988

"Radiation" 's ambiguous—*we*'re ambivalent—
    weighted toward horror—
        :   hardly hear "radiance"

Not *gemütlich* owl-light—*blinding* light—
    evanescent light like ours—us—ah!
        ugh!

Reflected light: tolerable light—
    only the crazy look at the sun minutes—hours
        no, it *don't* strengthen the eyes Mr. Yogi!

Dreamy dreamlight—refuge from *un*doing, *un*making light...
    Northern Lights—hah!—swirling i'th'empyrean—yick!
        we know what makes 'em tick!

Tock!
  talk!
        callous callous callous light careless light ach!

Cursed with a serious curse—oogh!—
    a discombobulating videocameraman—
        glowed like tungsten giving verse voice—oh!

Aurora borealis swooping i'th'bloody empyrean—hm?
    i'th'ionosphere's E region—*ja*?—particle rain
        from outer magnetosphere, mostly electrons—heh?

Seemed to be puttin' on a show for the hicks from Chicago
    but Robert Frost *was* a fairybaiter—yuck!—
        how did *he* know?

Northern Lights—*more* Northern Lights!
  them rays!
        all say oo! 'n' ah! seein' 'em slip 'n' slide

Took over the floor and gave voice—whew!
    flared every *which* way—anger—ecstasy–eros—
        the ol'-time sublime, eh Longinus?

'N' silly silly silliness, hebephrenic silliness, eh doc?
      muck! 'n' fuck! 'n' suck! 'n' fuck! 'n' muck!
            sudden sweetness, edge of oblivion, gone

Gone
            gone
                        gone

Gone
            gone
                        gone

Gone
            gone
                        gone

Not the end—
      Grandma brought Hermes Trismegistus to the West
            in a covered wagon...

CARBIDE=LAMP LIGHT

MASER LIGHT

EDITORIAL DEPARTMENT

PAYROLL DISTRIBUTION

A	R	C	M (TOTAL)	F (REF. EDIT)	W (NEW INTER YEAR BOOK)	O (NEW STAN YEAR BOO)
A	2	3	4	5	6	7
ARC=LIGHT	RADIANCE	CANDLE=LIGHT	MATCH=FLAME	ECLIPSE=LIGHT	WAXING LIGHT	OIL=LAMP LIGHT
AURORA BOREALIS	REFLECTED LIGHT	CHEMICAL LIGHT	MOON=LIGHT	EYE LIGHT	WANING LIGHT	OWL=LIGHT
ACTINIC RAYS	RAINBOW	CORAL LIGHT	MIDNIGHT SUN	ELECTRIC LIGHT	WATER LIGHTS	ORANGE LIGHT
AURORA	RED LIGHT	COLD LIGHT	MARSH LIGHT	EMERALD LIGHT	WILL-O'-THE-WISP	OLD LIGHT
AURORA AUSTRALIS	RUBY LIGHT	COLORED LIGHT	MERCURY=VAPOR LAMPLIGHT	EARTHLIGHT	WHITE LIGHT	ORGONE RADIATION
ATOM BOMB LIGHT	RADIATION	CINEMATOGRAPHIC LIGHT	MAROON LIGHT	ETHER	WHALE=OIL LAMPLIGHT	ORGONE LUMINAT
ARTIFICIAL LIGHT	RAYS OF LIGHT	CINEOGRAPHIC LIGHT	MAGIC FLAMES	ETHER LAMPLIGHT	WATCHING=CANDLE LIGHT	OUTDOOR FIRELIGH
ANNEALING=LAMPLIGHT	RAYS	CRESSET LIGHT	MAGIC LANTERN LIGHT	ELECTRIC ARC=LIGHT	WATCH=CANDLE LIGHT	OIL=GAS LIGHT
ALCOHOL LAMPLIGHT	READING=LAMPLIGHT	COOPER=HEWITT LAMPLIGHT	MAGNESIUM LIGHT	ELECTRIC LAMPLIGHT	WATCH=LIGHT	OLIVE=OIL LAMPLIGH
ARGAND LAMPLIGHT	ROOF=LAMPLIGHT	CLUTCH=LAMPLIGHT	MAGIC FIRELIGHT	ENAMELING=LAMPLIGHT	WOOD=OIL LAMP LIGHT	AMETHYST LIGHT
ADVANCING IGNITION	REICHSANSTALT'S LAMPLIGHT	CLEAR GRAY LIGHT	MINERS LAMPLIGHT	ENLIGHTENMENT	WINESTONES OIL LIGHT	AGATE LIGHT
AFTER-GLOW	ROSE LAMPLIGHT	CAMPFIRE LIGHT	MERCURY LAMPLIGHT	ELUCIDATION	WAXLIGHT LIGHT	ACHROITE LIGHT
AUFKLÄRUNG	ROSE LIGHT	CORUSCATION	MOONSHINE	EFFULGENCE	LUMINOUSNESS	ALEXANDRA LIGHT
AUREOLA	REFLECTED LIGHT	CAMPHOR=OIL LIGHT	MECHANICAL LAMP LIGHT	EARTH=SHINE	LUMMIFEROUSNESS	ALMANDIT LIGHT
AUREOLE	RADIOACTIVITY	CASTANHA=OIL LIGHT	MAKE=AND=BREAK IGNITER LIGHT	EXPLODING STARLIGHT	LAMBENCY	AMAZON STONE LIG
AZURE LIGHT	REFULGENCE	COCONUT=OIL CANDLELIGHT	MOON=BEAM	EXIT=LIGHT LIGHT	ROSEOPAL LIGHT	AMBER LIGHT
FLUMINOTHERMIC LIGHT	RESPLENDENCE	COLOR	MIDNIGHT OIL	EQUINOCTIAL LIGHT	MILKY WAY	AQUAMARINE LIGHT
ACETYLENE LIGHT	REFRACTED LIGHT	COMMON LIGHT	MELON=OIL LAMPLIGHT	EARLY LIGHT	SATELLITE LIGHT	OPALESCENT LIGHT
ACTINISM	RELUCENCE	CARNELIAN LIGHT	MUSTARD=OIL LIGHT	EVANESCENT LIGHT	MOVIE LIGHT	ORDINARY LIGHT
ANDAFOIL LIGHT	RHODOCHROSITE LIGHT	CARMINE LIGHT	(METEOR LIGHT)	EXTRA LIGHT	WINKING LIGHT	OPAL LIG

LASER LIGHT (crossed out)
LUMINOUSNESS
LUMINIFEROUSNESS
LAMBENCY

SPARK
IGNITERLIGHT   SPARKLING
SPARKS   SHEEN
WEEK ENDING SUNBEAM SCINTILLANCE
SUNSET   SOFT RADIANCE
SHINE   SEAL=OIL LAMPLIGHT

DICT'NARY				SHINING SCINTILLA	SUPERNOVA LIGHT	
L	**N**	**I**	**J**	**S**	**K**	**Z**
8	**9**	**10**	**J**	**Q**	**K**	**JOKERS**
LIGHT	NOON LIGHT	INCANDESCENCE	JACK=O'=LANTERN	SUN=LIGHT	KLIEG LIGHT	ZODIACAL LIGHT
LUCENCE	NORTHERN LIGHTS	IGNIS FATUUS	JEWEL LIGHT	STAR=LIGHT	KINDLING LIGHT	ZIRCON LIGHT
LAVENDER LIGHT	NIGHT LIGHT	INFRA=RED LIGHT	JADE LIGHT	ST. ELMO'S FIRE	KINETOSCOPIC LIGHT	ZINCZ LIGHT
LILAC LIGHT	NAPALM FLAME	INCANDESCENT LAMPLIGHT	JACK LIGHT	SPECTRUM	KINETOGRAPHIC LIGHT	SPARK
LEMON LIGHT	NEW LIGHT	ILLUMINATION	JALOUSIE LIGHT	SODIUM=VAPOR LAMPLIGHT	KINEMATOGRAPHIC LIGHT	SPARK IGNITER LIGHT
LUMINANCE	NERNST LAMP LIGHT	IRRADIATION	JAPANESE LANTERN LIGHT	SAPPHIRE LIGHT	KINEOGRAPHIC LIGHT	SUNBEAM
LUMINATION	NATURAL LIGHT	ICE=SKY LIGHT	JUMP=SPARK IGNITER LIGHT	SHIMMERING LIGHT	KEROSENE LIGHT	SUNSET
LUMINESCENCE	NORTH LIGHT	IGNITER LIGHT	JABLOCHKOFF IGNITER LIGHT	SHADED LIGHT	KEATS LAMPLIGHT	SHINE
LAMPLIGHT	NAPHTHA=LAMP LIGHT	IGNITION	JACK=LAMP LIGHT	SHIMMER	KITSON LAMPLIGHT	SUNRISE
LUMINOSITY	NITRO=FILLED LAMP LIGHT	ILLUCIDATION	JACK=O'=LANTERN LIGHT	STREET LAMPLIGHT (crossed out)	CRIMSON LIGHT	SHINING LIGHT / 5 TOP (crossed out)
LANTERN LIGHT	NOONTIDE =LIGHT	ILLUMINATING GASLIGHT	JACK=O'=WISP	SHINE SUN (crossed out)	CARBUNCLE LIGHT	SCINTILLA
LUSTER	NOON=TIDE	IRRIDESCENCE	JACK=LANTERN LIGHT	SHINING LIGHT	CAIRNGORM LIGHT	SPARKLE
LIGHT RAYS	NIMBUS	IRRIDESCENT LIGHT	JACKLIGHT LIGHT	SAFETY LAMPLIGHT (crossed out)	CHROME LIGHT	SPARKLING
LUMINIFEROUS ETHER	NOON=DAY	IOLITE LIGHT	JACINTH LIGHT	SATURN LIGHT (crossed out)	CANARY LIGHT	SHEEN
LIMELIGHT	NAKED LIGHT	INTELLECTUAL LIGHT	JADEITE LIGHT	SHADE	COMET LIGHT	SCINTILLANCE
LUMINESCENCE LAMPLIGHT	NEON LIGHT	INTUITIVE LIGHT	JASPER LIGHT	SHADOWY LIGHT	CLOUD LIGHT	SUPERNOVA (crossed out)
LIGHTNING	NOVA LIGHT	INFINITE LIGHT	JOYOUS LIGHT	SHADOWED LIGHT	COMA CLUSTER LIGHT	SEAL=OIL LAMPLIGHT
LIGHT OF DAY	NEPTUNE LIGHT	INNER LIGHT	CHANDELIER LIGHT	ST. GERMAIN LAMPLIGHT	CORONA CLUSTER LIGHT	SUNSTONE LIGHT
LAMBENT FLAME	MAGELLANIC CLOUD LIGHT	ICE LIGHT	CANDELA=BRA LIGHT	STUDENT=LAMP LIGHT	CITRINE LIGHT	SPOTLIGHT LIGHT (crossed out)
LUCIDITY	METEORITE LIGHT	ALTAR LIGHT	SEARCHLIGHT LIGHT	SMOKING=LAMPLIGHT	KLNX/SOLAR LIGHT	(crossed out)

Right margin: RED FANS · BLUE FANS · RED FLORAL · BLUE FLORAL · RED

Notes to Jackson Mac Low's *Complete Light Poems*

[The following notes include original commentary authored by Jackson Mac Low with editorial additions and acknowledgements by Anne Tardos and Michael O'Driscoll, registered in square brackets. Notes 1–22 were prepared by JML for the publication of *22 Light Poems* (Black Sparrow Press, 1968). Wherever possible, the editors have maintained JML's original account of his compositional practices, and otherwise cite the state of the copy text, anomalies, and previous publications.]

==

I've often been asked whether this or that Light Poem was composed by means of chance operations, & if so, how it was done. The fact is that I used many different methods, ranging from "pure" systematic chance to spontaneous expression, in writing these poems.

The Light Poems began in early June 1962 as a chart listing 280 names of kinds of light (plus 8 "extras"). Lettered roughly on a Funk and Wagnalls Editorial Department Payroll Distribution form, this chart has 14 columns & 20 rows. Each column is headed by one of the 14 letters contained in my name & that of my wife (Iris Lezak), & beneath each letter is the symbol of a playing-card denomination (Ace to King, plus Jokers). The letters appear in the order "A, R, C, M, E, W, O, L, N, I, J, S, K, Z." Some were undoubtedly assigned to denominations because they were the latter's symbols ("A" & "K"); I don't know how the others were assigned. While each light name on the chart begins with one of these letters, only 7 columns are filled solely with names beginning with the letters heading them. The lower rows of the others are mostly filled with names beginning with other chart letters (usually ones similar in sound), since I was able to think of, or find in dictionaries, too few beginning with some letters (e.g., "Z") & far more than 20 beginning with others (e.g., "S"). At first I listed extra light names as nearly above their initial letters as possible, but after shifting all but two extra "S" 's to the "Z" column, I filled the empty spaces in other columns with extras & ended with only 8 extra names listed solely above (a "C," an "M," 4 "L" 's, & 2 "S" 's). The following were the columns (extra names are printed above initial letters):

Light Poems Chart

CARBIDE-LAMPLIGHT

A	R	C
A	2	3
ARCHLIGHT	RADIANCE	CANDLE LIGHT
AURORA BOREALIS	REFLECTED LIGHT	CHEMICAL LIGHT
ACTINIC RAYS	RAINBOW	CORAL LIGHT
AURORA	RED LIGHT	COLD LIGHT
AURORA AUSTRALIS	RUBY LIGHT	COLORED LIGHT
ATOM BOMB LIGHT	RADIATION	CINEMATOGRAPHIC LIGHT
ARTIFICIAL LIGHT	RAYS OF LIGHT	CINEOGRAPHIC LIGHT
ANNEALING-LAMPLIGHT	RAYS	CRESSET LIGHT
ALCOHOL LAMPLIGHT	READING-LAMPLIGHT	COOPER-HEWITT LAMPLIGHT
ARGAND LAMPLIGHT	ROOF-LAMPLIGHT	CLUTCH-LAMPLIGHT
ADVANCING IGNITION	REICHSANSTALT'S LAMPLIGHT	CLEAR GRAY LIGHT
AFTERGLOW	ROSE LAMP LIGHT	CAMPFIRE LIGHT
AUFKLÄRUNG	ROSE LIGHT	CORUSCATION
AUREOLA	REFLECTED LIGHT	CAMPHOR-OIL LIGHT
AUREOLE	RADIOACTIVITY	CASTANHA-OIL LIGHT
AZURE LIGHT	REFULGENCE	COCONUT-OIL CANDLELIGHT
ALUMINOTHERMIC LIGHT	RESPLENDENCE	COLOR
ACETYLENE LIGHT	REFRACTED LIGHT	COMMON LIGHT
ACTINISM	RELUCENCE	CARNELIAN LIGHT
ANDA-OIL LIGHT	RHODOCHROSITE LIGHT	CARMINE LIGHT

O	L	N
7	8	9
OIL-LAMP LIGHT	LIGHT	NOON-LIGHT
OWL-LIGHT	LUCENCE	NORTHERN LIGHTS
ORANGE LIGHT	LAVENDER LIGHT	NIGHT-LIGHT
OLD LIGHT	LILAC LIGHT	NAPALM FLAME
ORGONE RADIATION	LEMON LIGHT	NEW LIGHT
ORGONE LUMINATION	LUMINANCE	NERNST LAMP LIGHT
OUTDOOR FIRELIGHT	LUMINATION	NATURAL LIGHT
OIL-GAS LIGHT	LUMINESCENCE	NORTH LIGHT
OLIVE-OIL LAMPLIGHT	LAMPLIGHT	NAPHTA-LAMP LIGHT
AMETHYST LIGHT	LUMINOSITY	NITRO-FILLED LAMP LIGHT
AGATE LIGHT	LANTERN LIGHT	NOONTIDE-LIGHT
ACHROITE LIGHT	LUSTER	NOONTIDE
ALEXADRITE LIGHT	LIGHT RAYS	NIMBUS
ALMANDITE LIGHT	LUMINIFEROUS ETHER	NOONDAY
AMAZONSTONE LIGHT	LIMELIGHT	NAKED LIGHT
AMBER LIGHT	LUMINESCENCE LAMPLIGHT	NEON LIGHT
AQUAMARINE LIGHT	LIGHTNING	NOVA LIGHT
OPALESCENT LIGHT	LIGHT OF DAY	NEPTUNE LIGHT
ORDINARY LIGHT	LAMBENT FLAME	MAGELLANIC CLOUD LIGHT
OPAL LIGHT	LUCIDITY	METEORITE LIGHT

MASER LIGHT

M	E	W
4	5	6
MATCHFLAME	ECLIPSE LIGHT	WAXING LIGHT
MOONLIGHT	EYE LIGHT	WANING LIGHT
MIDNIGHT SUN	ELECTRIC LIGHT	WATER LIGHTS
MARSH LIGHT	EMERALD LIGHT	WILL-O'-THE-WISP
MERCURY-VAPOR LAMPLIGHT	EARTHLIGHT	WHITE LIGHT
MAROON LIGHT	ETHER	WHALE-OIL LAMPLIGHT
MAGIC FLAMES	ETHER LAMPLIGHT	WATCHING-CANDLE LIGHT
MAGIC LANTERN LIGHT	ELECTRIC-ARC LIGHT	WATCH-CANDLE LIGHT
MAGNESIUM LIGHT	ELECTRIC LAMPLIGHT	WATCH-LIGHT
MAGIC FIRELIGHT	ENAMELING-LAMPLIGHT	WOOD-OIL LAMPLIGHT
MINERS' LAMPLIGHT	ENLIGHTENMENT	WINESTONES-OIL LIGHT
MERCURY LAMPLIGHT	ELUCIDATION	WAXLIGHT LIGHT
MOONSHINE	EFFULGENCE	LUMINOUSNESS
MECHANICAL LAMP LIGHT	EARTHSHINE	LUMINIFEROUSNESS
MAKE-AND-BRAKE IGNITER LIGHT	EXPLODING STARLIGHT	LAMBENCY
MOONBEAM	EXIT-LIGHT LIGHT	ROSE OPAL LIGHT
MIDNIGHT OIL	EQUINOCTIAL LIGHT	MILKY WAY
MELON-OIL LAMPLIGHT	EARLY LIGHT	SATELLITE LIGHT
MUSTARD-OIL LIGHT	EVANESCENT LIGHT	MOVIE LIGHT
METEOR LIGHT	EXTRA LIGHT	WINKING LIGHT

SOFT RADIANCE
SHINING

I	J	S
10	J	Q
INCANDESCENCE	JACK-O'-LANTERN	SUNLIGHT
IGNIS FATUUS	JEWEL LIGHT	STARLIGHT
INFRA-RED LIGHT	JADE LIGHT	ST. ELMO'S FIRE
INCANDESCENT LAMPLIGHT	JACK LIGHT	SPECTRUM
ILLUMINATION	JALOUSIE LIGHT	SODIUM-VAPOR LAMPLIGHT
IRRADIATION	JAPANESE LANTERN LIGHT	SAPPHIRE LIGHT
ICE-SKY LIGHT	JUMP-SPARK IGNITER LIGHT	SHIMMERING LIGHT
IGNITER LIGHT	JABLOCHKOFF IGNITER LIGHT	SHADED LIGHT
IGNITION	JACK-LAMP LIGHT	SHIMMER
ILLUCIDATION	JACK-O'-LANTERN LIGHT	STREET-LAMP LIGHT
ILLUMINATING GASLIGHT	JACK-O'-WISP	SUNSHINE
IRIDESCENCE	JACK-LANTERN LIGHT	SHINING LIGHT
IRIDESCENT LIGHT	JACK-LIGHT LIGHT	SAFETY-LAMP LIGHT
IOLITE LIGHT	JACINTH LIGHT	SATURN LIGHT
INTELLECTUAL LIGHT	JADEITE LIGHT	SHADE
INTUITIVE LIGHT	JASPER LIGHT	SHADOWY LIGHT
INFINITE LIGHT	JOYOUS LIGHT	SHADOWED LIGHT
INNER LIGHT	CHANDELIER LIGHT	ST. GERMAIN LAMPLIGHT
ICE LIGHT	CANDELABRA LIGHT	STUDENT-LAMP LIGHT
ALTAR LIGHT	SEARCHLIGHT LIGHT	SMOKING-LAMP LIGHT

K	Z				
K	JOKERS				
KLIEG LIGHT	ZODIACAL LIGHT	♠	1		
KINDLING LIGHT	ZIRCON LIGHT	♦	2	R*	F
KINETOSCOPIC LIGHT	ZINCZ LIGHT	♣	3	E / D	A
KINETOGRAPHIC LIGHT	SPARK	♥	4		N / S
KINEMATOGRAPHIC LIGHT	SPARK IGNITER LIGHT	♠	5		
KINEOGRAPHIC LIGHT	SUNBEAM	♦	6	B / L	F
KEROSENE LIGHT	SUNSET	♣	7	U / E	A
KEATS LAMPLIGHT	SHINE	♥	8		N / S
KITSON LAMPLIGHT	SUNRISE	♠	9		F
CRIMSON LIGHT	STOPLIGHT LIGHT	♦	10	R	L / O
CARBUNCLE LIGHT	SCINTILLA	♣	11	E / D	R
CAIRNGORM LIGHT	SPARKLE	♥	12		A / L
CHROME LIGHT	SPARKLING	♠	13		F
CANARY LIGHT	SHEEN	♦	14	B	L / O
COMET LIGHT	SCINTILLANCE	♣	15	L / U / E	R
CLOUD LIGHT	SUPERNOVA LIGHT	♥	16		A / L
COMA CLUSTER LIGHT	SEAL-OIL LAMPLIGHT	♠	17		
CORONA CLUSTER LIGHT	SUNSTONE LIGHT	♦	18	R	
CITRINE LIGHT	SPOTLIGHT LIGHT	♣	19	E / D	
KINDLY LIGHT	SOLAR LIGHT	♥	20		

*Words printed vertically formed a single column of letters and stood for the colors and patterns on the backs of five packs of playing cards that were shuffled together. The numbers were mainly used in conjunction with the RAND Corporation's A Million Random Digits with 100,000 Normal Deviates (Glencoe, IL: The Free Press, 1955).

The light names are hyphenated & spaced as they appear on the chart; I'd probably do it differently today. I deliberately made the chart very hastily, with a few hasty revisions, and accepted many partial redundancies. The chart was first set up to be used with 5 differently-backed packs of cards, so that suit & back were to decide the row, denomination the column, of each light name used. However, the Light Poems were actually composed in many different ways.

1ˢᵗ Light Poem

Only the 1ˢᵗ Light Poem was composed solely by drawing light names from the chart by chance operations. I forget why 4 light names were taken from one column each time during composition of the 1ˢᵗ.

[This poem appeared previously in *Pogamoggan* 1, eds. Harry Lewis, Leonard Neufeld, Robert Shatkin (Brooklyn, NY: 1964); *22 Light Poems* (Los Angeles: Black Sparrow Press, 1968); *Representative Works* (New York: Roof Books, 1986).]

2ⁿᵈ Light Poem

In the 2ⁿᵈ, only light names beginning with letters in Diane Wakoski's name were chance-drawn from the chart. In addition, phrases were drawn from a story fragment on the back of a magazine clipping (a "girlie" picture, I think) sent me by the collagist Ray Johnson. While chance means determined which source (chart or clipping) was drawn from each time, & the light names & phrases appear in the order drawn, the sentences & verse lines in which they appear were freely composed.

[This poem appeared previously in *Joglars* 1.2, ed. Clark Coolidge & Michael Palmer (Providence, 1964); *22 Light Poems* (Los Angeles: Black Sparrow Press, 1968); *Representative Works* (New York: Roof Books, 1986).]

3ʳᵈ Light Poem

The composition of the 3ʳᵈ involved no chance means. All light names in it were chosen from the chart in the order in which they appear in the poem.

[This poem appeared previously in *East Side Review* 1, ed. SS. Sherbell (New York: 1966); *22 Light Poems* (Los Angeles: Black Sparrow Press, 1968); *Representative Works* (New York: Roof Books, 1986).]

4th Light Poem

The 4th begins with a light name from the chart which I'm pretty sure I didn't draw by chance. The rest of the poem was composed without chance means.

[This poem appeared previously in *Dream Sheet*, ed. Diane Wakoski (New York: 1965); *22 Light Poems* (Los Angeles: Black Sparrow Press, 1968).]

5th Light Poem

The 5th (which is also a performance piece that I hope some reader will perform some time—Geo. Brecht never has) was freely composed except for the list of light names, which was drawn from the chart by means of cards & random digits.

[This poem appeared previously in *East Side Review* 1, ed. SS. Sherbell (New York: 1966); *22 Light Poems* (Los Angeles: Black Sparrow Press, 1968).]

6th Light Poem

The 6th contains only light names beginning with the letters in "Carol Bergé." Chance determined which letter begins the light name in each line. When the letter was on the chart, chance means drew the light. When it wasn't, I wrote the first one, beginning with that letter, that came into my head. Otherwise the lines were written freely, somewhat "automatically," & rapidly.

[This poem appeared previously in *East Side Review* 1, ed. SS. Sherbell (New York: 1966); *22 Light Poems* (Los Angeles: Black Sparrow Press, 1968).]

7th Light Poem

In writing the 7th, I began to use as a supplementary source a numerology booklet entitled *Your Lucky Number*. Chance determined which source was drawn from each time. Triplets of random digits drew phrases from the booklet; cards & random-digit couplets drew light names from the chart. Connecting words & verse lines were freely composed, but indentations were usually determined by placing a letter (or whole word) in one line directly under its appearance in a line (not necessarily the preceding one) above it.

[This poem appeared previously in *Joglars* 1.2, ed. Clark Coolidge & Michael Palmer

(Providence, 1964); *22 Light Poems* (Los Angeles: Black Sparrow Press, 1968); *Representative Works* (New York: Roof Books, 1986).]

8th Light Poem

In composing the 8th (which is also a play that I hope Dick Higgins & Alison Knowles, or maybe someone else, will perform some day), chance means drew light names from the chart & a few lucky-number phrases. Connecting material was freely composed. Vertical line-ups of letters & words usually determined indentations.

[This poem appeared previously in *22 Light Poems* (Los Angeles: Black Sparrow Press, 1968).]

9th Light Poem

The "new" 9th is not meant to imply that I condone either the violence of the Algerian Revolution or the authoritarianism of the present Algerian government. (I don't.) Nevertheless, their Light Poem is their Revolution. The "abandoned" 9th was a long prose meditation involving chance-drawn light names & autobiographical associations that wandered endlessly.

[This poem appeared previously in *22 Light Poems* (Los Angeles: Black Sparrow Press, 1968).]

10th Light Poem

The 10th is composed entirely of chance-drawn light names and lucky-number phrases.

[This poem appeared previously in *Joglars* 1.2, ed. Clark Coolidge & Michael Palmer (Providence, 1964); *22 Light Poems* (Los Angeles: Black Sparrow Press, 1968); *Thing of Beauty*, ed. Anne Tardos (Berkeley, Los Angeles: University of California Press, 2008.

11th Light Poem

The 11th incorporates at the start a few chance-drawn light names that begin with letters in "Richard Maxfield," but then proceeds associatively with details & quoted passages from an account of a Paris fire found in Roger Shattuck's *The Banquet Years* (New York, 1961).

[This poem appeared previously in *East Side Review* 1, ed. SS. Sherbell (New York: 1966); *22 Light Poems* (Los Angeles: Black Sparrow Press, 1968).]

12ᵗʰ Light Poem

In composing the 12ᵗʰ, I used chance means to draw light names & lucky-number phrases in the order in which they appear, but the material connecting them was composed freely.

[This poem appeared previously in *August Light Poems* as *Caterpillar* IX, ed. Clayton Eshleman (New York, 1967); *22 Light Poems* (Los Angeles: Black Sparrow Press, 1968).]

13ᵗʰ Light Poem

The 13ᵗʰ was composed rapidly & freely with no chance means.

[This poem appeared previously in *August Light Poems* as *Caterpillar* IX, ed. Clayton Eshleman (New York, 1967); *22 Light Poems* (Los Angeles: Black Sparrow Press, 1968); *Thing of Beauty*, ed. Anne Tardos (Berkeley, Los Angeles: University of California Press, 2008).]

14ᵗʰ Light Poem

The 14ᵗʰ was composed as the 12ᵗʰ was. In addition, lines 2 thru 5 were drawn from somewhere in the Old Testament. In poems of this sort, long free sections often connect the gifts of chance. The latter act as "jets": they boost the poem along as rocket firings do space ships.

[This poem appeared previously in *Poems from the Floating World* 5, ed. Jerome Rothenberg (New York: Hawk's Well Press, 1963); *August Light Poems* as *Caterpillar* IX, ed. Clayton Eshleman (New York, 1967); *22 Light Poems* (Los Angeles: Black Sparrow Press, 1968); *Representative Works* (New York: Roof Books, 1986).]

15ᵗʰ Light Poem

Both the light names & most of the other words in the 15ᵗʰ were given by chance. In fact, the system used to get the "other words" was so intricate that I tired of it & abandoned the poem. However, rereading it a year or so later, I found this "abandoned fragment" was a complete poem that spoke to me with great urgency.

[This poem appeared previously in *August Light Poems* as *Caterpillar* IX, ed. Clayton Eshleman (New York, 1967); *22 Light Poems* (Los Angeles: Black Sparrow Press, 1968).]

16th Light Poem

The 16th was composed freely in reaction to the incident mentioned & without use of chance or chart.

[This poem appeared previously in *August Light Poems* as *Caterpillar* IX, ed. Clayton Eshleman (New York, 1967); *22 Light Poems* (Los Angeles: Black Sparrow Press, 1968); *Thing of Beauty*, ed. Anne Tardos (Berkeley, Los Angeles: University of California Press, 2008).]

17th Light Poem

I forget what went wrong with the abandoned 17th, but between its abandonment & the present, Paul Williams composed his own light poem: a series of incredibly delicate kinetic sculptures incorporating electric light (often many very small bulbs) in various ways.

[This poem appeared previously in *22 Light Poems* (Los Angeles: Black Sparrow Press, 1968).]

18th Light Poem

In the 18th, part *I* was composed freely; some of the words in part *II* were given by chance; & all of the "cuc . . ." words in part *III* were drawn from a chance-determined page of a dictionary.

[This poem appeared previously in *22 Light Poems* (Los Angeles: Black Sparrow Press, 1968).]

19th Light Poem

The 19th is a "2nd-generation" chance poem produced by the same method as that used in making "Alarm Clock" (published in the 2nd *Insect Trust Gazette*). Its source is "Asymmetry 98," my first "environmental asymmetry," composed by first noticing something in the environment, writing its name, & then spelling it out in an initial-letter acrostic (working both horizontally & vertically) consisting of names of other things, persons, sounds, inner sensations, &c., noticed during composition. At each moment, the first thing I noticed that had the proper initial letter entered the poem. Lines ended when the notebook-page edge was reached, & were indented (the first word in indented lines beginning directly under the second in unindented lines) within horizontal spell-outs. All the words that spell out the first word are spelled out in successive lines. Words recur when letters recur. Only 15 different words appear in

ASYMMETRY 98

pillow Iris light light osculation
     watersound

Iris red Iris suede

light Iris green heels tape-recorder

light Iris green heels tape-recorder

osculation suede ceiling underwear
        light ache tape-recorder
        Iris red Iris suede
        osculation suede ceiling
        underwear neck

watersound ache tape-recorder envelope red
      suede osculation under-
          wear neck dog

The empty spaces in "Asymmetries" are notations for silences lasting at least as long as it would take the reader to say the words printed directly above or below them. Whole "lines of silence" occur between horizontal spell-outs (i.e., before each unindented line). Some or all of the silences may be replaced by sustained instrumental tones of the same duration. (See "Methods for Reading Asymmetries," *An Anthology*, ed. La Monte Young, New York, 1963.)

Early in 1963 I began composing by "thru-acrostic chance selection"—beginning with one word as key & taking subsequent words from a text as they spell out the key word by having that word's letters in corresponding places. Applying the method to "Asymmetry

98" (as I applied it to "Asymmetry 100" to produce "Alarm Clock"), I first spelled out "pillow" with subsequent words in the poem: "pillow light pillow heels pillow under-wear." The 2nd line spells out "light," the 2nd word in the 1st line, the 3rd line the 3rd word, &c. Thus the successive lines spell out the successive words of the lines above them with appropriate words from "Asymmetry 98" in the order in which I found them by repeated-ly reading thru the source poem. Line endings were produced by endings of words spelled out, by hyphens in "A. 98" (e.g. in spelling out "underwear" for line 6, the "`e'-in-the-4th-place" word reached in "A. 98" was the hyphenated "under-/wear"), & by my handwriting coming too near to the right edge of the notebook page to put another word on the line. At least two errors—my not noticing until 22 lines from the end that "dog" can give the "g" in "light" & my writing "light" 4 rather than 5 times in the next line—were accepted as part of the generative process. The only choices involved were those of source and method.

[This poem appeared previously in *FUCK YOU: A Magazine of the Arts* 5.3, ed. Ed Sand-ers (New York: 1963); *22 Light Poems* (Los Angeles: Black Sparrow Press, 1968).]

20th Light Poem

In composing the 20th, I reverted to the chart, drawing a small group of light names from it & later bringing them in again & again by use of cards (as told in the poem). However, I think I was mistaken when I wrote that I had found 13 light names up to that point. I must have realized this & added a few more light names before "closing" the set & using playing cards to bring only light names from the set into the poem from then on (begin-ning with part II). Besides using chance operations to bring in light names, I used a wide gamut of other procedures, ranging from free association to spontaneous selection of "found" passages from English and French dictionaries, an astronomy book, & the patter of the classical disc jockey Bill Watson (of WNCN-FM, New York), whose program was on the radio all during the long night of the poem's composition. Thus while systematic chance operations were used extensively in its composition, the 20th, in its all-over struc-ture, is a kind of "action" poem, drawing its elements—light names, "found" passages, thoughts, memories, &c., from both the inner & outer environments, & passing freely between association, elegy, reflection, narration, and exposition.

[This poem appeared previously in *22 Light Poems* (Los Angeles: Black Sparrow Press, 1968).]

21st Light Poem

The 21st was a surprise. It came while I was typing this note: I noticed that quite a few light names on the chart appear in none of the poems. I decided to write a Light Poem for the publisher of this book [*22 Light Poems*, Black Sparrow Press, 1968], John Martin, thinking that an unused light name might appear in it. However, the first letter of his name & the random-digit couplet 14 gave me "jacinth light," which already appears in the 12th. Realizing that I didn't know then (if I ever did) what "jacinth" means, I looked it up in the dictionary & the dictionary took over. Everything past the light name is "found" poetry. All dictionary line endings & punctuation caused line endings in the poem; otherwise, I ended lines when I pleased. Driven from definition to definition by "see"'s & "cf."'s ("confer"'s), I found the poem ending naturally with definitions of "catharsis."

[This poem appeared previously in *22 Light Poems* (Los Angeles: Black Sparrow Press, 1968).]

22nd Light Poem

The 22nd also happened while I was writing this note—because David Antin telephoned from California & because I'd been reading his new *Code of Flag Behavior*. The letters of the dedicatees' names, ordered as in the title, drew light names. When a letter was on the chart, a random-digit couplet drew a light name from its column. If it wasn't, the letter drew one from the "lamp" entry in the old *Funk & Wagnalls Standard* used in making the chart. Random digits were also used to draw linguistic terms from a photo copy of the glossary of W. Nelson Francis's *The Structure of American English* (New York: Ronald Press,, 1958).

[This poem appeared previously in *22 Light Poems* (Los Angeles: Black Sparrow Press, 1968); *Thing of Beauty*, ed. Anne Tardos (Berkeley, Los Angeles: University of California Press, 2008).]

23rd Light Poem

[This poem appeared previously as a single sheet folio with multicolored graphic by Ian Tyson (London: Tetrad Press, 1969).]

24th Light Poem

[This poem appeared previously in *Maps* 3, ed. John Taggart (Syracuse, NY: Syracuse University Press, n.d.).
25th Light Poem

[Previously unpublished: text based on MS and TS at Mandeville Special Collections Library, University of California, San Diego.]

26th Light Poem

[Previously unpublished: text based on MS and TS at Mandeville Special Collections Library, UCSD.]

27th Light Poem

[This poem appeared previously in *Vort* 8, ed. Barry Alpert (Silver Spring, MD: Vort Works Ink, 1975).]

28th Light Poem

[This poem appeared previously in *Caterpillar* XIII, ed. Clayton Eshleman (New York: 1970).]

29th Light Poem

[Previously unpublished: text based on MS and TS at Mandeville Special Collections Library, UCSD. See also Mac Low's note that directly follows the poem.]

30th Light Poem

[Previously unpublished: text based on TS at Mandeville Special Collections Library, UCSD.]

31st Light Poem

[Previously unpublished in print form: text based on MS at Mandeville Special Collections Library, UCSD. Published on audio cassette, *Black Box* 1 (Washington, DC, 1976).]

32nd Light Poem ("For the O & the B Stars)

[There are two 32nd Light Poems. This one is previously unpublished: text based on TS at Mandeville Special Collections Library, UCSD. The Editors located several identical copies of page one in typescript only, and no further evidence of additional text. The first page of the TS concludes with an indication of a strophe break, and so presumably the draft was intended to continue. However, because an additional, and entirely distinct, 32nd Light Poem was written, edited, and published in memory of Paul Blackburn, JML presumably abandoned this early version without plans to see it through to publication.]

32nd Light Poem (In Memoriam Paul Blackburn)

[This poem appeared previously in *Representative Works* (New York: Roof Books, 1986); *Jacket* 12, ed. John Tranter (Balmain, NSW: 2000); *Thing of Beauty*, ed. Anne Tardos (Berkeley, Los Angeles: University of California Press, 2008).]

33rd Light Poem

[Previously unpublished: text based on MS and TS at Mandeville Special Collections Library, UCSD.]

34th Light Poem

[Previously unpublished: text based on MS at Mandeville Special Collections Library, UCSD.]

35th Light Poem

[JML wrestled with the complex process of drafting this Light Poem as a script for performance. The manuscript includes an initial and incomplete attempt, which has not been included here. Several minor silent corrections have also been made. Previously unpublished: text based on MS at Mandeville Special Collections Library, UCSD.]

36th Light Poem

[This poem appeared previously as a chapbook published by Permanent Press, Number 5, "on the occasion of JML's first English Tour," (London: 1975); *Representative Works* (New York: Roof Books, 1986); *Thing of Beauty*, ed. Anne Tardos (Berkeley, Los Angeles: University of California Press, 2008).]

37th – 39th Light Poems

[Previously unpublished: text based on MS at Mandeville Special Collections Library, UCSD.]

40th Light Poem

[JML's manuscript notebook numbers this poem as the 39th. However, on the page previous to the draft, JML himself questions the numbering, asking "Is there a 40th Light Poem?" Because there is a 39th Light Poem extant (although unfinished), and because there is no 40th Light Poem that we have been able to identify, the Editors have renumbered this poem as the 40th Light Poem. We have been unable to locate the notebook indicated by JML at the point that the text breaks off. Previously unpublished: text based on MS at Mandeville Special Collections Library, UCSD.]

41st Light Poem

[Previously unpublished as complete: text based on MS and TS at Mandeville Special Collections Library, UCSD. Typescript includes only sections 1–11, 29–30. Sections 28, 29, & 30 appeared previously in *American Poetry Review* 4.2 (Philadelphia: 1975).]

42nd Light Poem

[Previously unpublished: text based on TS at Mandeville Special Collections Library, UCSD. JML made explicit attempts to publish this poem in both *Poetry* and *The Virginia Quarterly Review*.]

43rd – 47th Light Poems

[Previously unpublished: text based on MS at Mandeville Special Collections Library, UCSD.]

48th Light Poem

[This poem appeared previously in *Margins* 24, ed. Tom Montag (Milwaukee: 1975).]

49th Light Poem

[Previously unpublished: text based on TS at Mandeville Special Collections Library, UCSD.]

50th Light Poem

[Previously unpublished: text based on MS at Mandeville Special Collections Library, UCSD.]

51st Light Poem

[Previously unpublished: text based on TS at Mandeville Special Collections Library, UCSD.]

52nd Light Poem

[Previously unpublished: text based on TS at Mandeville Special Collections Library, UCSD.]

53rd Light Poem

[There are two extant typescripts of this poem. The first, dated December 12–13, 1976, was subject to corrections by hand on several occasions over the next fourteen months, up until February 21, 1978. On retyping the poem one week later, JML concluded with the text as republished here, excluding four and a half additional pages of writing. Previously unpublished: text based on TS at Mandeville Special Collections Library, UCSD.]

54th Light Poem
[This poem appeared previously as a single sheet folio published by Membrane Press

(Milwaukee: 1978). For JML's production and performances notes, see the extended text that precedes the poem here, also as published in *Doings: Assorted Performance Pieces 1955–2002.* (New York: Granary Books, 2005).]

55th Light Poem

[No 55th Light Poem has been identified. JML seems to have lost track of his numbering. In the subsequent Light Poem he writes: "The first Light Poem in nearly a year—I hope it really *is* the / 56th."]

56th Light Poem

[This poem appeared previously in *Representative Works* (New York: Roof Books, 1986).]

57th Light Poem

[This poem appeared previously in *Paper Air* 2.1, ed. Gil Ott (Blue Bell, PA: 1979); *Representative Works* (New York: Roof Books, 1986); *Thing of Beauty*, ed. Anne Tardos (Berkeley, Los Angeles: University of California Press, 2008).]

58th Light Poem

[This poem appeared previously in *Representative Works* (New York: Roof Books, 1986); *Thing of Beauty*, ed. Anne Tardos (Berkeley, Los Angeles: University of California Press, 2008).]

59th Light Poem

[This poem appeared previously in *Bloomsday* (New York: Roof Books, 1986); *Postmodern American Poetry: A Norton Anthology* 2nd Edition, ed. Paul Hoover (New York: WW Norton, 2013).]

60th Light Poem

[This poem appeared previously in *Sulfur* 24, ed. Clayton Eshleman (Ypsilanti, MI: 1989).]